1 MONTH OF
FREE
READING

at

www.ForgottenBooks.com

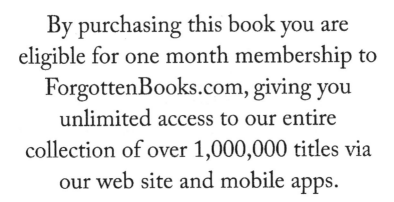

By purchasing this book you are eligible for one month membership to ForgottenBooks.com, giving you unlimited access to our entire collection of over 1,000,000 titles via our web site and mobile apps.

To claim your free month visit:

www.forgottenbooks.com/free1061218

ISBN 978-0-331-71664-1
PIBN 11061218

This book is a reproduction of an important historical work. Forgotten Books uses
state-of-the-art technology to digitally reconstruct the work, preserving the original format
whilst repairing imperfections present in the aged copy. In rare cases, an imperfection in
the original, such as a blemish or missing page, may be replicated in our edition. We do,
however, repair the vast majority of imperfections successfully; any imperfections that
remain are intentionally left to preserve the state of such historical works.

A LIST OF
AMERICAN DOCTORAL DISSERTATIONS
PRINTED IN 1918

PREPARED BY

KATHARINE JACOBS

CATALOGUE DIVISION

WASHINGTON
GOVERNMENT PRINTING OFFICE
1921

PREFATORY NOTE

The following list of theses (1918) has been compiled according to the plan adopted for the list of 1912, in which the method and arrangement are explained on pages 7 to 9 of the introduction by Mr. Charles A. Flagg. Theses received before November 1, 1920, are included in this list; theses received later will appear as a supplement to the list for 1919.

Supplementary lists of theses printed in 1914, 1916, and 1917 are prefixed. They are numbered continuously with the lists of 1914, 1916, and 1917 and distinguished in the subject index (Section III) by the addition of the date.

KATHARINE JACOBS

In Charge of Theses, Catalogue Division

HERBERT PUTNAM

    Librarian of Congress
Washington, D. C., November, 1920

CONTENTS

5

SUPPLEMENTARY LISTS OF THESES PRINTED IN 1914, 1916, AND 1917

(Received too late for 1914, 1916, and 1917 lists)

FOURTH SUPPLEMENTARY LIST OF THESES PRINTED IN 1914

(In continuation of first, second, and third supplementary lists prefixed to Lists of Theses printed in 1915, 1916, and 1917)

319 **Harmon, Esther,** 1880–

Johanna Schopenhauer . . . München, Kgl. hof-buchdr. Kastner & Callwey, 1914. 115 p.; 1 l.

Bryn Mawr college, 1912, PH. D.

"Ein abschnitt derselben unter dem titel 'Johanna Schopenhauer als schriftstellerin' erschien 1910 in dem 'Journal of English and Germanic philology,' vol. 9, nr. 2, 1910."

20–17030   PT2508.S6Z6

D

SECOND SUPPLEMENTARY LIST OF THESES PRINTED IN 1916

(In continuation of first supplementary list prefixed to List of Theses printed in 1917)

395 **Clark, Helen**, 1890–

    Visual imagery and attention: an analytical study . . . [Worcester, Mass., 1916] 2 p. l., p. [461]–492, 1 l.

University of Illinois, 1916, PH. D.
With a t.-p. and Contents [1918?] prefixed.
"Reprinted from the American journal of psychology, October, 1916, vol. xxvii."
18–16485   BF321.C6

396 **Coulter, Ellis Merton**, 1890–

    Effects of secession upon the commerce of the Mississippi Valley . . . [Cedar Rapids, 1916] cover-title, 1 p. l., p. [275]–300.

University of Wisconsin, 1917,   , PH. D.
Thesis note stamped on cover.
"Reprinted from the Mississippi Valley historical review, vol. iii, no. 3, Dec. 1916."
20–1138   HF3155.C6

397 **Ferguson, Maxwell**, 1888–

    State regulation of railroads in the South . . . New York, 1916. 2 p. l., 7–230 p.

Columbia university,   , PH. D.
Published also as Studies in history, economics and public law, ed. by the Faculty of political science of Columbia university. v. 67, no. 2; whole no. 162.
16–14676   HE1051.F4

398 **Harris, Lynn Harold**, *ed.*

    . . . Catiline his conspiracy, by Ben Jonson, ed., with introduction, notes and glossary, by Lynn Harold Harris . . . New Haven, Yale university press; [etc., etc.] 1916. lxi, 236 p.

(Yale studies in English, A. S. Cook, editor. liii)
Yale university, 1914, PH. D.
With reproduction of original t.-p.
20–11097   PR2608.A2H3

399 Hufford, Mason Edward.

The diffraction ring pattern in the shadow of a circular object . . .   [Lancaster, Pa., and Ithaca, N. Y., 1916] cover-title, p. [545]–550.

Indiana university, 1916, PH. D.

Without thesis note.

"Reprinted from the Physical review, n. s., vol. VII, no. 5, May, 1916."

20–8446   QC415.H8

400 Luckey, Bertha Musson.

The specific brightness of colors . . .   Lincoln, 1916. 60 p.

University of Nebraska, 1916, PH. D.

20–18162   QC495.L89

SUPPLEMENTARY LIST OF THESES PRINTED IN 1917

369 Blankenagel, John Carl.

. . . The attitude of Heinrich von Kleist toward the problems of life . . . Göttingen, Vandenholck & Ruprecht; Baltimore, The Johns Hopkins press, 1917. 2 p. l., 84 p.

(Hesperia; schriften zur germanischen philologie . . . nr. 9)
University of Wisconsin, 1915, PH. D.
Thesis note stamped on cover.
20–19790   PD25.H5nr.9

370 Dodson, John Dillingham.

An experimental study of the relative values of reward and punishment in habit formation . . . [Baltimore, 1917] cover-title, p. 231–276.

University of Minnesota, 1918, PH. D.
On cover: Department of psychology, April, 1918.
"Reprinted from Psychobiology, vol. I, no. 3, November 1917."
19–14375   QL751.D6

371 Jackson, Thomas Franklin.

The description and stratigraphic relationships of fossil plants from the lower Pennsylvania rocks of Indiana . . . [Indianapolis, 1917] p. 405–428.

Indiana university, 1916, PH. D.
Without thesis note.
Reprinted from the Proceedings of the Indiana academy of science, 1916.
20–18161   QE937.I6J2

372 Keddy, John Lewis, 1891–

The New York state legislative budget for 1917 . . . [New York, 1917] 2 p. l., iii–x, 141 p.

Columbia university, 1919, PH. D.
Published also as Municipal research, issued by the Bureau of municipal research, no. 86, June, 1917.
20–6668   HJ2053.N7K4

12

373 **Nichols, Harold William.**
. . . Theory of variable dynamical electrical systems . . . [Lancaster, Pa., Press of the New era printing company, 1917]   1 p. l., p. 171–193, 1 l.

University of Chicago, 1919, PH. D.
"Private edition, distributed by the University of Chicago libraries, Chicago, Illinois."
"Reprinted from the Physical review, n. s., vol. 10, no. 2, August, 1917."

20–2515   QC631.N65

374 **Spring, Evelyn.**
A study of exposition in Greek tragedy . . . [Boston, 1917]   1 p. l., p. 135–224.

"This essay in its original form, entitled Quo modo Aeschylus in tragoediis suis res antecedentis exposuerit, was presented in 1915 in partial fulfilment of the requirements for the degree of doctor of philosophy in Radcliffe college."
"Printed from the Harvard studies in classical philology, vol. XXVIII, 1917."

20–2140   PA3131.S7

SECTION 1

ALPHABETICAL LIST OF THESES PRINTED
IN 1918

ALPHABETICAL LIST OF THESES PRINTED IN 1918

1 **Abbott, Raymond Barrington,** 1873–

Law of motion of a droplet moving with variable velocity in air . . . Lancaster, Pa., Press of the New era printing company [1913] 1 p. l., p. [381]–395.

University of California, 1919, PH. D:
"Reprinted from the Physical review, n. s., vol. XII, no. 5, November, 1918."
19–14373 QA929.A2

2 **Adamson, William Augustus,** 1883–

2, 4-dihydroxybenzoyltetrachloro-o-benzoic acid and 2, 3, 4-trichloro-6-hydroxyxanthone-1-carboxylic acid and some of their derivatives, by W. R. Orndorff and W. A. Adamson . . . [Easton, Pa., 1918] 1 p. l., p. [1235]–1257.

"A reprint of an article based upon a thesis submitted to the Faculty of the Graduate school of Cornell university for the degree of doctor of philosophy, by William Augustus Adamson, 1917."
W. R. Orndorff, instructor under whom thesis was written.
"Reprinted from the Journal of the American chemical society, vol. XL, no. 8. August, 1918."
19–8336 QD341.A2O75

3 **Adkins, Homer Burton,** 1892–

The oxidation by means of alkaline potassium permanganate of acetaldehyde glycol, glycollic aldehyde, glyoxal, glycollic and glyoxalic acids . . . Columbus, O., 1918. 32 p.

Ohio state university, 1918, PH. D.
20–27008 QD281.O9A3

4 **Alexander, Thomas,** 1887–

The Prussian elementary schools . . . New York, The Macmillan company, 1918. viii p., 1 l., 571 p.

(*Lettered on cover:* Text-book series in education)
Columbia university, 1918, PH. D.
Thesis note attached to t.-p.
18–2687 LA724.A6

5 **Amy, Ernest Francis,** 1884–
The text of Chaucer's Legend of good women . . .
Princeton, Princeton university press; [etc., etc.] 1918.
ix, 109 p.

Princeton university, 1914, PH. D.
18–10198   PR1882.A5

6 **Andrews, John Bertram,** 1880–
Nationalisation (1860–1877) . . .

(*In* Commons, J. R. History of labour in the United States.
New York, 1918.   vol. II, pt. 5, p. 1–191)
University of Wisconsin, 1908, PH. D.
Without thesis note.

HD8066.C7   vol. II, pt. 5

7 **Armstrong, A. Joseph.**
. . . Operatic performances in England before Handel . . .   Waco, Tex. [Baylor university press] 1918.
74 p.

University of Pennsylvania, 1908, PH. D.
"Baylor university bulletin [vol. XXI] no. 4."
18–22832   ML1731.2.A76

8 **Aronberg, Lester.**
. . . Note on the spectrum of the isotopes of lead.
The structure of the bismuth line   4722 . . .   [Chicago,
1918]   1 p. l., p. 96–103.

University of Chicago, 1917, PH. D.
"Private edition, distributed by the University of Chicago
libraries, Chicago, Illinois."
"Reprinted from the Astrophysical journal, vol. XLVII, no. 2,
March, 1918."
18–11724   QC462.L4A8

9 **Artschwager, Ernst Friedrich,** 1889–
Anatomy of the potato plant, with special reference
to the ontogeny of the vascular system . . .   [Wash-
ington, D. C., 1918]   1 p. l., p. 221–252.

Cornell university, 1918, PH. D.
"Reprinted from Journal of agricultural research, vol. XIV, no. 6,
Washington, D. C., August 5, 1918."
19–16516   QK643.P7A7

10 **Atwell, Wayne Jason,** 1889–
The development of the hypophysis cerebri of the
rabbit (*Lepus cuniculus* L.) . . . Philadelphia [1918]
1 p. l., p. 271–337.

University of Michigan, 1917, PH. D.
"Reprinted from the American journal of anatomy, vol. 24, no. 3,
September, 1918."
"Author's abstract of this paper issued by the [Wistar institute]
Bibliographic service, July 19."
19–2854   QL868.A7

11 **Ayres, Clarence Edwin.**
. . . The nature of the relationship between ethics
and economics . . . Chicago, Ill., The University of
Chicago press, 1918. 1 p. l., v–ix, 58 p.

University of Chicago, 1917, PH. D.
"Philosophic studies no. 8."
18–22529   BJ53.A82

12 **Bakke, Arthur Laurence.**
. . . Determination of wilting . . . [Chicago, 1918]
1 p. l., p. 81–116.

University of Chicago, 1917, PH. D.
"Private edition, distributed by the University of Chicago
libraries, Chicago, Illinois."
"Reprinted from the Botanical gazette, vol. LXVI, no. 2, August,
1918."
"Contributions from the Hull botanical laboratory 241."
19–221   QK873.B3

13 **Baldwin, Francis Marsh,** 1885–
Pharyngeal derivatives of *Amblystoma* . . . Philadelphia, 1918. 1 p. l., 605–680 p., 1 l.

University of Illinois, 1917, PH. D.
"Author's abstract of this paper issued by the [Wistar institute]
Bibliographic service, March 2."
"Contributions from the Zoological laboratories of the University
of Illinois, no. 103."
"Reprinted from the Journal of morphology, vol. 30, no. 2, March,
1918."
18–27181   QL668.C2B25

14 **Baldwin, Thomas Whitfield,** 1890– *ed.*
An edition of Philip Massinger's Duke of Milan . . .
by Thomas Whitfield Baldwin . . . Lancaster, Pa.,
Press of the New era printing company, 1918. ix, 197 p.

Princeton university, 1916, PH. D.
With reproduction of t.-p.: The Dvke of Millaine. A tragædie.
As it hath beene often acted by his Majesties seruants, at the blacke
Friers. Written by Philip Massinger gent. London, Print<t>ed
by B. A. for Edward Blackmore, 1623.
19–116   PR2704.D8 1918

15 **Balz, Albert George Adam,** 1887–
Idea and essence in the philosophies of Hobbes and
Spinoza . . . New York, Columbia university press,
1918. 2 p. l., 86 p., 1 l.

Columbia university, 1916, PH. D.
Published also as Archives of philosophy, no. 10.
18–8201   B3998.B32

16 **Barnes, Harry Elmer,** 1889–
A history of the penal, reformatory and correctional
institutions of the state of New Jersey, analytical and
documentary . . . Trenton, N. J., MacCrellish & Quigley company, 1918. 654 p., 1 l.

Columbia university, 1918, PH. D.
18–11733   HV9475.N5B3

17 **Barron, Mary Louise,** 1892–
. . . State regulation of the securities of railroads
and public service companies . . . Philadelphia, 1918.
28 p.

University of Pennsylvania, 1917, PH. D.
"Reprinted from vol. LXXVI of the Annals of the American
academy of political and social science."
18–11198   HE2236.B3

18 **Barrows, Albert Lloyd,** 1883–
The significance of the skeletal variations in the
genus *Peridinium* . . . [Berkeley, 1918] cover-title,
[397]–478, [1] p.

University of California, 1917, PH. D.
University of California publications in zoology, v. 18, no. 15,
June 27, 1918, with a special thesis t.-p. dated May 1917 attached
to the cover-title.
18–20526   QL368.D6B3

19 **Bast, Victor,** 1883–
   The action of calcium carbide òn benzaldehyde and
   on some other organic compounds . . . [Washington,
   D. C.] Catholic university of America, 1918.   93 p.
   Catholic university of America, 1918, PH. D.
   20–1824   QD181.C2B3

20 **Beardslee, John Walter,** 1879–
   . . . The use of φύσις in fifth-century Greek literature
   . . . Chicago, Ill., The University of Chicago press,
   1918.   v, 126 p.
   University of Chicago, 1913, PH. D. '
   18–6672   PA427.B4

21 **Beatty, Albert James,** 1871–
   A comparative study of corporation schools as to their
   organization, administration, and methods of instruction . . . [Urbana ? 1918]   116 p.
   University of Illinois, 1917, PH. D.
   18–27260   T73.B4

22 **Beckerman, Harry.**
   . . . I. Tungsten hexabromide. II. Tungsten complexes . . . Philadelphia, Pa., 1918.   19 p.
   University of Pennsylvania, 1918, PH. D.
   18–14652   QD181.W1B4

23 **Beckwith, Martha Warren,** 1871–   *tr.*
   The Hawaiian romance of Laieikawai with introduc-
   tion and translation by Martha Warren Beckwith . . .
   Washington, Govt. print. off., 1918.   384 p.
   Columbia university, 1918, PH. D.
   Slip with thesis note mounted on t.-p.
   "Translated from the Hawaiian text of S. N. Haleole (printed in
   Honolulu, 1863)"
   "Reprinted from the Thirty-third annual report of the Bureau of
   American ethnology."
   18–26566   PL6448.5.L3   1918

24 **Beegle, Frank Moore,** 1889–
   A study of the mutarotation of glucose and fructose
   . . . New York, 1918.   21, [1] p.
   Columbia university, 1918, PH. D.
   19–16517   QD321.B4

25 **Behre, Ellinor Helene.**
. . . An expérimental study of acclimation to temperature in *Planaria dorotocephala* . . . [Lancaster, Pa., Press of the New era printing company, 1918] 1 p. l., p. 277–317.

University of Chicago, 1918, PH. D.

"Private edition, distributed by the University of Chicago libraries, Chicago, Illinois."

"Reprinted from Biological bulletin, vol. xxxv., no. 5, November, 1918."

19–3160   QL391.T9B3

26 **Benda, Theodore.**
Mental factors in the causation, cure and prevention of disease . . . [Worcester ? Mass., 1918]   90 p.

Clark university, 1917, PH. D.

19–97   BF173.B4

27 **Bichowsky, Francis Russell von.**
Equilibrium in the reaction between water and sulfur at high temperatures. The dissociation of hydrogen sulfide . . . [Easton, Pa., 1918]   cover-title, p. [368]–375.

University of California, 1916, PH. D.

Thesis t.-p. attached to cover of the issue, by Merle Randall and F. Russell v. Bichowsky, which was reprinted from the Journal of the American chemical society, vol. XL, no. 2, February, 1918.

20–6557   QD501.B58

28 **Blanchard, Julian,** 1885–
The brightness sensibility of the retina . . . Lancaster, Pa., Press of the New era printing company, 1918. 1 p. l., 81–99, [1] p.

Columbia university, 1917, PH. D.

"Reprinted from the Physical review, vol. XI, no. 2, February, 1918."

"Communication no. 45 from the research laboratory of the Eastman kodak company."

18–7762   QP481.B6

29 **Blancké, Wilton Wallace.**
. . . The dramatic values in Plautus . . . [Geneva, N. Y., Press of W. F. Humphrey] 1918.   69 p.

University of Pennsylvania, 1916, PH. D.

18–22818   PA

30 **Blechman, Nathan.**
The philosophic function of value; a study of experience showing the ultimate meaning of evolution to be
the attainment of personality through culture and religion . . .   Boston, R. G. Badger [°1918]   3 p. l., v–xv p.,
1 l., 15–148 p.

(*Lettered on cover:* Studies in philosophy)
New York university, 1917, PH. D.
Thesis note on verso of t.-p.
18–9758   BD232.B5

31 **Blumberg, Alfred.**
Studies in immunity with special reference to complement fixation . . .   Washington, D. C. [1918]   cover-
title, 11, [1] p.

George Washington university, 1917, PH. D.
"Reprint from the Journal of laboratory and clinical medicine,
vol. III, no. 7, April, 1918."
20–5880   QR185.B5

32 **Bock, Carl William,** 1888–
The association of voluntary movements . . .   [Balti-
more, 1918]   1 p. l., p. 277–318, 1 l.

Ohio state university, 1917, PH. D.
"Reprinted from Psychobiology, vol. I, no. 4, January, 1918."
19–16514   BF295.B6

33 **Bonns, Walter Weidenfeld,** 1877–
. . . Etherization of tissues and its effect on enzyme activity . . .   [St. Louis, 1918]   cover-title,
p. 225–299.

(Washington university doctoral dissertations)
Washington university, St. Louis, 1918, PH. D.
"Publications of Washington university, Saint Louis, series v,
number 29."
"Reprinted from Annals of the Missouri botanical garden, November, 1918, vol. v, no. 4."
19–2852   QK896.B6

34 **Bossard, James Herbert.**
. . . The churches of Allentown; a study in statistics . . .   Allentown, Pa., Jacks, the printer, 1918.
116 p.

University of Pennsylvania, 1918, PH. D.
18–15647   BR560.A35B7

35 **Boström, Otto Henry**, 1889–

. . . Alternative readings in the Hebrew of the books of Samuel . . . Pub. by the authority of the Board of directors of Augustana college and theological seminary, Rock Island, Illinois. Rock Island, Ill., Augustana book concern, printers, 1918. 60 p.

(Augustana library publications no. 8)
Yale university, 1916, PH. D.
Without thesis note.
18–8964   BS1322.B7

36 **Bovard, John Freeman**, 1881–

The transmission of nervous impulses in relation to locomotion in the earthworm . . . [Berkeley, 1918] 2 pt.

University of California, 1917, PH. D.
University of California publications in zoology, v. 18, nos. 7, 8, with a special thesis t.-p. dated May, 1917, attached to the cover-title of [pt. 1]
[Pt. 2] has title: The function of the giant fibers in earthworms.
18–19474   .   QL391.O4B55

37 **Bowen, Ray Preston**, 1882–

The novels of Ferdinand Fabre, including an account of his life and a discussion of his position in literature . . . Boston, R. G. Badger [1918]   138 p., 1 l.

(*Half-title:* Studies in literature)
Cornell university, 1916, PH. D.
Published also without thesis note.
20–89   PQ2241.F3Z6   1918a

38 **Bowman, Howard Hiestand Minnich**, 1886–

Ecology and physiology of the red mangrove . . . Philadelphia, 1918.   1 p. l., p. [589]–673.

University of Pennsylvania, 1917, PH. D.
"Reprinted from Proceedings American philosophical society, vol. LVI, 1917."
18–3802   QK495.M28B6

39 **Boyce, Mryna M.**

The diplomatic relations of England with the Quadruple alliance 1815–1830. [Iowa City? 1918]   76 p.

University of Iowa, 1917, PH. D.
Published also as University of Iowa monographs, 1st ser., no. 22, November 1918.
19–10367   D383.B6

40 **Bradley, Harriett,** 1892–
The enclosures in England, an economic reconstruction . . . New York, 1918. 3 p. l., 9–113 p.
Columbia university, 1917, PH. D.
Published also as Studies in history, economics and public law, ed. by the Faculty of political science of Columbia university, vol. LXXX, no. 2, whole no. 186.
18–22990   HD594.6.B83

41 **Bramble, Charles Clinton,** 1890–
A collineation group isomorphic with the group of the double tangents of the plant quartic . . . [Baltimore, 1918] 1 p. l., [351]–365 p., 1 l.
Johns Hopkins university, 1917, PH. D.
"Reprinted from American journal of mathematics, vol. XL, no. 4, October, 1918."
18–22840   QA601.B77

42 **Brandenburg, George Clinton.**
Psychological aspects of language . . . [Baltimore, 1918] cover-title, p. 313–332.
University of Wisconsin, 1915, PH. D.
Thesis note stamped on cover.
"Reprint from the Journal of educational psychology, vol. IX, no. 6, June, 1918."
20–2742   LB1139.L3B7

43 **Brann, Albert.**
. . . On the preparation of formamide . . . [Easton, Pa., 1918] cover-title, p. [793]–796.
University of Wisconsin, 1918, PH. D.
Part I of thesis.
Thesis note stamped on cover; also found in a foot-note on p. [793]
"Reprinted from the Journal of the American chemical society, vol. XL, no. 5, May, 1918."
                                              QD305.A7B7

Brann, Albert.
. . . The effect of dissolved substances on the velocity of crystallization of water . . . [Easton, Pa., 1918] cover-title, p. [1168]–1184.
University of Wisconsin, 1918, PH. D.
Part II of thesis.
Thesis note stamped on cover; also found in a foot-note on p. [1168]
"Reprinted from the Journal of the American chemical society, vol. XL, no. 8, August, 1918."
                                              QD305.A7B7

Brann, Albert.

. . . The effect of dissolved substances on the velocity of crystallization of formamide . . . [Easton, Pa., 1918] cover-title, p. [1184]–1187.

University of Wisconsin, 1918, PH. D.
Part III of thesis.
Thesis note is found in a foot-note on p. [1184]
"Reprinted from the Journal of the American chemical society, vol. XL, no. 8, August, 1918."

QD305.A7B7

44 Brede, Charles Frederic.

. . . The German drama in English on the Philadelphia stage from 1794 to 1830 . . . Philadelphia, Americana Germanica press, 1918.   5 p. l., 3–295 p.

(*Half-title:* Americana Germanica.   [no. 34])
University of Pennsylvania, 1905, PH. D.
Published also without thesis note.
18–19316   PN2277.P5B72

45 Breitenbecher, Joseph Kumler.

. . . The relation of water to the behavior of the potato beetle in a desert . . . [Washington, 1918] 2 p. l., p. 343–384.

University of Chicago, 1913, PH. D.
"Private edition, distributed by the University of Chicago libraries, Chicago, Illinois."
"Reprinted from Publication 263 of the Carnegie institution of Washington."
19–12709   SB945.P68B7

46 Bridgman, J. Allington, 1892–
Gallium . . . [Easton, Pa., 1918]   33 p.

Cornell university, 1917, PH. D.
"Reprinted from the Journal of the American chemical society, vol. XL, no. 10, October, 1918."
19–7993   QD181.G2B7

47 Bridgman, Olga Louise, 1886–
An experimental study of abnormal children, with special reference to the problems of dependency and delinquency . . . [Berkeley, 1918]   cover-title, 59 p.

University of California, 1915, PH. D.
University of California publications in psychology, v. 3, no. 1, March 30, 1918, with a special thesis t.-p. dated May, 1915, attached to the cover-title.
18–20534   LB1121.B66

48 Brighton, Thomas Bow, 1887-

The free energy of formation of cyanide ion and of hydro-cyanic acid . . . [Easton, Pa., 1918] cover-title, p. [482]-489.

University of California, 1917, PH. D.

Thesis t.-p. attached to the cover of the reprint from the Journal of the American chemical society, vol. XL, no. 3, March, 1918, which has title: The oxidizing power of cyanates and the free energy of formation of cyanides, by Gilbert N. Lewis and Thomas B. Brighton.

18-17014   QD181.C15B7

49 Brockbank, Thomas William.

Redintegration in the albino rat, a study in retention . . . Washington, D. C., 1918. 2 p. l., 66 p.

Catholic university of America, 1918, PH. D.

Published also as Behavior monographs, v. 4, no. 2, serial no. 18.

19-15473   QL785.B7

50 Broderick, Thomas M., 1889-

The relation of the titaniferous magnetite deposits of northeastern Minnesota to the Duluth gabbro . . . Lancaster, Pa., Press of the New era printing company, 1918. 1 p. l., p. 663-696, 35-49.

University of Minnesota, 1917, PH.D.

Reprinted from Economic geology, vol. XII, no. 8, December, 1917; vol. XIII, no. 1, January, 1918.

18-13677   TN403.M6B7

51 Brown, Thomas Benjamin, 1892-

Kathodo-fluorescence of crystals, by Thomas B. Brown. Part I.—A quantitative investigation of the kathodo-fluorescence of willemite, kunzite, and soda glass. (A description of the results obtained by J. A. Veazey.) Part II.—A further investigation of willemite by the writer . . . Lancaster, Pa., Press of the New era printing company, 1918. 1 p. l., p. [39]-57.

"Part I is the substance of a thesis presented to the Faculty of the Graduate school of Cornell university by J. A. Veazey for the degree of doctor of philosophy."

"Part II is a thesis presented to the Faculty of the Graduate school of Cornell university by Thomas B. Brown for the degree of doctor of philosophy." 1916.

"Since the untimely death of J. A. Veazey prevented the immediate publication of his thesis, and since the work of the writer is so closely related to this previous work, these two papers are here issued as a single publication."

"Reprinted from Physical review, vol. XI, no. 1, January, 1918."

18-14649   QC477.B75

52 Bruce, Harold Lawton, 1887–

. . . Voltaire on the English stage . . . Berkeley, University of California press [1918] cover-title, p. [1]–152.

(University of California publications in modern philology. v. 8, no. 1)

"This study is the revision of a thesis of the same title submitted in 1915 to the faculty of the graduate school of Yale university in candidacy for the degree of doctor of philosophy."—Pref.

A 18–763   PQ2123.B8

53 Buchholz, John Theodore.

. . . Suspensor and early embryo of *Pinus* . . . [Chicago; 1918]   1 p. l., p. 185–228.

University of Chicago, 1917, PH. D.

"Private edition, distributed by the University of Chicago libraries, Chicago, Illinois."

"Reprinted from the Botanical gazette, vol. LXVI, no. 3, September, 1918."

"Contributions from the Hull botanical laboratory 242."

18–22455   QK643.P6B8

54 Burchett, Bessie Rebecca.

. . . Janus in Roman life and cult, a study in Roman religions . . . Menasha, Wis., George Banta publishing company, 1918.   4 p. l., 75 p.

University of Pennsylvania, 1913, PH. D.

19–2404   BL820.J2B8

55 Burwash, Edward Moore Jackson, 1873–

. . . The geology of Vancouver and vicinity . . . Chicago, Ill., The University of Chicago press, 1918. 3 p. l., 3–106 p.

University of Chicago, 1915, PH. D.

18–23456   QE187.B87

56 Butterworth, Julian Edward.

. . . Problems in state high school finance . . . Yonkers-on-Hudson, N. Y., World book company, 1918. ix, 214 p.

(School efficiency monographs)

University of Iowa, 1911, PH. D.

Without thesis note.

18–12356   LB1620.B8

57 **Campbell, Ivy Gertrude.**

Manaism; a study in the psychology of religion . . . [Worcester, 1918]   1 p. l., 49 p.

Clark university, 1914, PH. D.
"Reprinted from the American journal of psychology, January, 1918, vol. XXIX."
19-2459   GN471.C3

58 **Campion, John Leo,** 1884–

Das verwandtschaftsverhältnis der handschriften des Tristan Ulrichs von Türheim, nebst einer probe des kritischen textes . . .   Baltimore, J. H. Furst company, 1918.   1 p. l., 42 p., 1 l.

Johns Hopkins university, 1917, PH. D.
Reprinted from Studies in philology, vol. XV, no. 1, January, 1918, p. 23–64.
18-8294   PT1661.U5C3

59 **Carsner, Eubanks.**

Angular-leafspot of cucumber: dissemination, over-wintering and control . . .   Washington, Govt. print. off., 1918.   cover-title, p. 201–220, 3 l.

University of Wisconsin, 1917, PH. D.
Thesis note stamped on cover.
"Reprinted from Journal of agricultural research, vol. XV, no. 3 . . . October 21, 1918."
20-1832   SB608.C88C3

60 **Chang, Tso-Shuen.**

History and analysis of the commission and city-manager plans of municipal government in the United States . . .   Iowa City, Ia., 1918.   290 p.

Iowa university, 1917, PH. D.
Published also as University of Iowa monograph. 1st ser., no. 18, July 1918.   Studies in the social sciences, v. 1.
19-10378   JS342.C42

61 **Chapman, Royal Norton,** 1889–

The basal connections of the tracheae of the wings of insects . . .   Ithaca, N. Y., The Comstock publishing company, 1918.   1 p. l., p. 27–51.

Cornell university, 1917, PH. D.
"Reprinted from The wings of insects by John Henry Comstock."
19-7992   QL847.C4

62 **Chen, Phoo Hwa,** 1889–

An investigation of comparative deflections of steel arch ribs with three, two, and no hinges . . . [Ithaca, N. Y., 1918] 2 p. l., 24 p.

Cornell university, 1917, PH. D.
Abstract of thesis.
"Reprinted from the Cornell civil engineer, vol. XXVI. pp. 184, 229, Feb., Mar., 1918."
18–15120   TG327.C5

63 **Childs, Hubert Guy,** 1871–

An investigation of certain phases of the reorganization movement in the grammar grades of Indiana public schools . . . Fort Wayne, Ind., Fort Wayne printing co., 1918. viii, 187 p., 1 l.

Columbia university, 1918, PH. D.
Published also without thesis note.
18–15791   LA283.C53

64 **Clark, Guy Wendell,** 1887–

The properties and composition of oocytin . . . [Baltimore, The Waverly press] 1918. cover-title, p. 253–262.

University of California, 1918, PH. D.
Reprint from the Journal of biological chemistry, vol. XXXV, no. 2, August, 1918, with a special thesis t.-p. dated June, 1918, attached to the cover-title.
19–8250   QP91.C55

65 **Clothier, Robert Waitman,** 1871–

Farm organization in the irrigated valleys of southern Arizona . . . [Washington, D. C., 1918] cover-title, 4, 59, [1], 13, [1] p.

George Washington university, 1917, PH. D.
A reissue of United States Department of agriculture Bulletin no. 654, June 14, 1918, with 2 preliminary leaves and Addenda: Review of literature bearing on the subject (13, [1] p.)
18–23714   S615.C58

66 **Cohn, Edwin Joseph.**

. . . Studies in the physiology of spermatozoa . . . [Lancaster, Pa., 1918] 1 p. l., p. 167–218.

University of Chicago, 1917, PH. D.
"Private edition, distributed by the University of Chicago libraries, Chicago, Illinois."
"Reprinted from Biological bulletin, vol. XXXIV, no. 3, March, 1918."
18–20896   QP255.C6

67 **Cole, Howard Irving**, 1892–

The use of textile fibers in microscopic qualitative chemical analysis . . . [Easton, Pa., 1917–18] 1 p. l. 7, 7 p.

Cornell university, 1917, PH. D.

"Reprinted from the Journal of industrial and engineering chemistry, vol. 9, no. 10, page 969. October, 1917; vol. 10, no. 1, page 48. January, 1918."

18–7764   QD81.C6

68 **Coombs, Helen Copeland**, 1891–

The relation of the dorsal roots of the spinal nerves and the mesencephalon to the control of the respiratory movements . . . [Boston, 1918] 1 p. l., p. 459–471, 1 l.

Columbia university, 1918, PH. D.

"Reprinted from the American journal of physiology, vol. xlvi, July, 1918."

18–23724   QP121.C7

69 **Cornell, Clare Brown**.

"A graduated scale for determining mental age" . . . [Frankfort, Ky., State journal co., 1918] 41 p.

University of Nebraska, 1915, PH. D.

20–1885   LB1131.C55

70 **Cornell, Ethel Letitia**, 1892–

A new clinical test for temperature sensitivity, a contribution to the study of temperature reaction in nervous diseases based on the reaction to simultaneous cold and hot stimulation . . . New York, P. B. Hoeber, 1918. 1 p. l., 119–158, 335–372 p., 1 l.

Columbia university, 1919, PH. D.

"Reprinted from vol. i, no. 3 . . . and vol. i, no. 9 . . . The Neurological bulletin . . . °1918."

19–8248   QP391.C8

71 **Cotterill, Robert Spencer**, 1884–

Southern railroads and western trade, 1840–1850.

(*In* Mississippi Valley historical review. Cedar Rapids, Ia., 1917. vol. iii, no. 4, p. [427]–441)

University of Wisconsin, 1919, PH. D.

Part i of thesis.

Without thesis note.

F351.M69   v. 3, no. 4

Cotterill, Robert Spencer, 1884–
Memphis railroad convention, 1849.

(*In* Tennessee historical magazine, Nashville, 1918. vol. 4, no. 2, p. [83]–94)
University of Wisconsin, 1919, PH. D.
Part II of thesis.
Without thesis note.

F431.T28 v. 4, no. 2

Cotterill, Robert Spencer, 1884–
The national railroad convention · in St. Louis, 1849 . . .

(*In* Missouri historical review. Columbia, 1918. vol. XII, no. 4, p. 203–215)
University of Wisconsin, 1919, PH. D.
Part III of thesis.
Without thesis note.

F461.M59 v. 12, no. 4

72 **Crooker, Sylvan Jay,** 1893–
. . . Influence of a series spark on the direct current corona . . . [New Haven, 1918] 1 p. l., p. 281–300, 1 l.
University of Illinois, 1917, PH. D.
"Reprinted from the American journal of science, vol. XLV, April, 1918."
18–19476

QC643.C7

73 **Curtis, George Morris,** 1890–
The morphology of the mammalian seminiferous tubule . . . Philadelphia [1918] 1 p. l., p. 339–394.
University of Michigan, 1914, PH. D.
"Reprinted from the American journal of anatomy, vol. 24, no. 3, September, 1918."
"Author's abstract of this paper issued by the [Wistar institute] Bibliographic service, July 19."
19–4496

QL878.C8

74 **Curtis, Otis Freeman,** 1888–
Stimulation of root growth in cuttings by treatment with chemical compounds . . . [Ithaca, 1918] 1 p. l., p. 71–138.
Cornell university, 1916, PH. D.
"Reprinted from Memoir no. 14, August, 1918, of Cornell university agricultural experiment station."
19–16684

QK746.C8 1918

75 **Davidson, Gordon Charles,** 1884–
The North West company . . . [Berkeley, 1918]
cover-title, xi, 349 p.

University of California, 1916, PH. D.
University of California publications in history, vol. VII, with a
special thesis t.-p., dated 1916, attached to the cover-title.
19–10399   F1060.4D26

76 **Davidson, Joseph George,** 1892–
The formation of aromatic hydrocarbons from natural
gas condensate . . . New York city, 1918. 37, [1] p.

Columbia university, 1918, PH. D.
19–4927   QD341.H9D25

77 **Davis, Elmer Fred,** 1887–
Rocks of the Franciscan group. 1. The sandstone.
2. The radiolarian cherts . . . [Berkeley, 1918] 2 pt.

University of California, 1917, PH. D.
University of California publications, Bulletin of the Department
of geology, v. 11, nos. 1 and 3, with a special thesis t.-p. attached to
the cover of [pt. 1]
19–3247   QE445.D3

78 **Dawson, Andrew Ignatius,** 1876–
Variations in bacteria caused by change of medium
. . . [New York?] 1918. 2 p. l., 15, [1] p.

Columbia university, 1918, PH. D.
18–14655   QR84.D3

79 **De Porte, Joseph Vital,** 1889–
Irrational involutions on algebraic curves . . .
[Baltimore, 1918] 1 p. l., p. [47]–68.

Cornell university, 1916, PH. D.
"Reprinted from American journal of mathematics, vol. XL, no. 1,
January, 1918."
13–7756   QA603.D4

80 **Derieux, John Bewley.**
. . . The use of mercury drops in Millikan's experiment. Photoelectric effects on mercury droplets . . .
[Lancaster, Pa., and Ithaca, N. Y., 1918] 1 p. l.,
[203]–226, [1], [276]–284 p.

University of Chicago, 1919, PH. D.
"Private edition, distributed by the University of Chicago
libraries, Chicago, Illinois."
"Reprinted from the Physical review, n. s., vol. XI, nos. 3 and 4,
March and April, 1918."
19–16524   QC721.D4
33564°—21——3

81 **Dodds, Harold Willis,** 1889–.

. . . Procedure in state legislatures . . . Philadelphia, The American academy of political and social science, 1918. vi, 112 p.

University of Pennsylvania, 1917, PH. D.
Published also as Supplement no. 1 to the Annals of the American academy of political and social science, May, 1918.
18–15635   JK2488.D7   1918a

82 **Douglas, Gertrude Elizabeth,** 1883–

A study of development in the family *Agaricaceae.* Part I: A study of development in the genus *Cortinarius.* Part II: The development of some exogenous species of agarics . . . [Lancaster, Pa., 1916–18] 1 p. l., p. 319–335, [35]–54.

Cornell university, 1917, PH. D.
"Reprinted from Am. jour. bot., vol. 3: June 1916 . . . vol. 5: Jan. 1918."
18–13249   QK629.A4D7

83 **Dudgeon, Winfield Scott.**

. . . Morphology of *Rumex crispus* . . . [Chicago, 1918] 1 p. l., p. 393–420.

University of Chicago, 1917, PH. D.
"Private edition, distributed by the University of Chicago libraries, Chicago, Illinois."
"Reprinted from the Botanical gazette, vol. LXVI, no. 5, November 1918."
"Contributions from the Hull botanical laboratory 244."
19–860   QK495.R95D8

84 **Dunbar, Carl Owen.**

. . . Stratigraphy and correlation of the Devonian of western Tennessee . . . [New Haven, 1918] cover-title, p. 732–756.

Yale university, 1917, PH. D.
Abstract of thesis.
"Contributions from the Paleontological laboratory, Peabody museum, Yale university, New Haven, Conn., U. S. A."
"From the American journal of science, vol. XLVI, December, 1918."
20–3170   QE665.D8

85 **Dushkin, Alexander Mordecai,** 1890–
Jewish education in New York city . . .   New York,
The Bureau of Jewish education, 1918.   2 p. l., ix p.,
1 l., 559 p., 1 l.

Columbia university, 1918, PH. D.
19–14029   LC743.N5D8

86 **Eastman, Ermon Dwight,** 1891–
The measurement of low temperatures and the
measurement of specific heats between 60 degrees and
300 degrees absolute . . .   [Easton, Pa., 1918]   cover-
title, p. [489]–500.

University of California, 1917, PH. D.
Thesis t.-p. attached to the cover of the reprint from the Journal
of the American chemical society, vol. XL, no. 3, March, 1918, which
has title: The specific heats at low temperatures of sodium, potassium,
magnesium and calcium metals, and of lead sulfide, by E. D. Eastman and W. H. Rodebush.
18–17855   QC295.E3

87 **Eberson, Frederick,** 1892–
A bacteriologic study of the diphtheroid organisms
with special reference to Hodgkin's disease . . .   New
York city, 1918.   56 p.

Columbia university, 1918, PH. D.
18–23723   QR201.D6E3

88 **Eller, William Henri.**
Ibsen in Germany, 1870–1900 . . .   Boston, R. G.
Badger [ᶜ1918]   203 p.

(*Lettered on cover:* Studies in literature)
"The greater part of the following investigation was presented to
the Graduate school at the University of Wisconsin, 1916, in partial
fulfillment of the requirements for the degree of doctor of philosophy."—Pref.
Thesis note stamped on t.-p.
19–1737   PT8900.G3E4

89 **Ellinger, Esther Parker.**
The southern war poetry of the civil war . . .
Philadelphia, Pa. [Hershey, Pa., The Hershey press]
1918.   192 p.

University of Pennsylvania, 1918, PH. D.
18–18349   PS261.E5

90 **Ellingwood, Albert Russell.**
. . . Departmental coöperation in state government
. . . Menasha, Wis., George Banta publishing com-
pany, 1918. 6 p. l., 300 p.

University of Pennsylvania, 1918, PH. D.
Published also without thesis note.
18–16361   JK2525.E53

91 **Engelhardt, Nickolaus Louis,** 1882–
A school building program for cities . . . New
York city, Teachers college, Columbia university, 1918.
ix, 130 p., 1 l.

Columbia university, 1918, PH. D.
Published also as Contributions to education, Teachers college,
Columbia university, no. 96.
19–4101   LB3209.E7

92 **Essenberg, Christine Elizabeth,** 1879–
The factors controlling the distribution of the *Poly-*
noidae of the Pacific coast of North America . . .
[Berkeley, 1918]   cover-title, p. [171]–238.

University of California, 1917, PH. D.
University of California publications in zoology, v. 18, no. 11,
March 8, 1918, with a special thesis t.-p. dated May, 1917, attached
to the cover-title.
18–15672   QL391.P9E762

93 **Estcourt, Rowland Metzner,** 1855–
The conflict of tax laws . . . [Berkeley, 1918]
cover-title, p. [115]–231.

University of California, 1916, PH. D.
University of California publications in economics, v. 4, no. 3,
April 2, 1918, with a special thesis t.-p. attached to the cover-title.
18–15634   HJ2377.E7

94 **Faust, Ernest Carroll,** 1890–
Life history studies on Montana trematodes . . .
[Urbana, 1918]   120 p., 1 l.

University of Illinois, 1917, PH. D.
"Reprinted from the Illinois biological monographs, vol. 4: 1–120."
18–27127   QL391.T7F3   1918 a

95 **Felsing, William August,** 1891–
   I. The equilibrium of the reaction $Ag_2S + H_2 = 2Ag + H_2S$. II. The equation of state of ether vapor . . .
   [Cambridge, Mass.] Technology press, 1918.   39 p.

   Massachusetts institute of technology, 1918, PH. D.
   Abstract of thesis.
   19–19964   QD501.F36

96 **Fenton, Frederick Azel,** 1893–
   The parasites of leaf-hoppers, with special reference
   to biology of the *Anteoninae* . . . [Columbus, O.]
   1918.   cover-title, [84] p.

   (Ohio state university. Contributions from the Department of
   zoology and entomology. no. 51)
   Ohio state university, 1918, PH. D.
   Without thesis note.
   Reprinted from the Ohio journal of science, vol. XVIII, no. 6, p.
   177–212; no. 7, p. 243–278; no. 8, p. 285–296.
   A 19–97   SB945.L5F3

97 **Florence, Philip Sargant,** 1890–
   Use of factory statistics in the investigation of indus-
   trial fatigue, a manual for field research . . . New
   York, 1918.   156 p.

   Columbia university, 1918, PH. D.
   Published also as Studies in history, economics and public law,
   ed. by the Faculty of political science of Columbia university. vol.
   LXXXI, no. 3; whole no. 190.
   18–20899   HD7261.F62

98 **Folsom, Donald.**
   The influence of certain environmental conditions, especially water supply, upon form and structure in *Ranunculus* . . . [Baltimore, 1918] 1 p. l., p. 209–276.

   University of Minnesota, 1917, PH. D.
   "Reprinted from Physiological researches, vol. 2, no. 5, December,
   1918."
   19–3245   QK495.R21F6

99 **Foote, Paul Darwin,** 1888–
   Some characteristics of the Marvin pyrheliometer . .
   [Washington, 1918]   cover-title, 1 p. l., p. 605–634.

   University of Minnesota, 1917, PH. D.
   Issued also as Scientific papers no. 323 of the Bureau of standards.
   This issue is identical with that, with the addition of a cover-title.
   19–14378   QC912.F62

100 **Fortune, Alonzo Willard.**
. . . The conception of authority in the Pauline writings . . . Chicago, Ill., 1918. 2 p. l., 183 p.

> University of Chicago, 1915, PH. D.
> "Private edition, distributed by the University of Chicago libraries."
> 18–5880   BS2655.A8F6

101 **Foster, Finley Melville Kendall,** 1892–
English translations from the Greek; a bibliographical survey . . . New York, Columbia university press, 1918. xxix, 146 p., 1 l.

> (*Half-title:* Columbia university studies in English and comparative literature)
> Columbia university, 1918, PH. D.
> Published also without thesis note.
> 19–3880   Z7018.T7E71

102 **Fox, Dixon Ryan,** 1887–
The decline of aristocracy in the politics of New York . . . New York, 1918. xiii, 460 p., 1 l.

> Columbia university, 1917, PH. D.
> Published also as Studies in history, economics and public law, ed. by the Faculty of political science of Columbia university, vol. LXXXVI, whole no. 198.
> 19–16519   F123.F79

103 **Freas, Raymond,** 1886–
Esterification limits of benzoic and toluic acids with lower alcohols . . . Easton, Pa., Eschenbach printing co., 1918. 14 p., 1 l.

> Johns Hopkins university, 1917, PH. D.
> 18–14651   QD341.A2F78

104 **Freed, Edgar Stanley,** 1899–
I. A thermodynamic investigation of reactions involving silver sulfide and silver iodide. II. The equilibrium between nitric oxide, nitrogen, peroxide, and aqueous solutions of nitric acid . . . [Cambridge, Mass.] Technology press, 1918. 16 p.

> Massachusetts institute of technology, 1918, PH. D.
> Abstract of thesis.
> 19–20158   QD501.F77

105 **Friedline, Cora Louisa,** 1893–
The discrimination of cutaneous patterns below the
two-point limen . . . [Worcester, 1918] 1 p.l., p. 400–
419.

Cornell university, 1918, PH. D. ·
"Reprinted from the American journal of psychology, October,
1918, vol. XXIX."
19–15845   QP451.F9

106 **Fukuya, Shoan Masuzo.**
. . . An experimental study of attention from the
standpoint of mental efficiency: a contribution to educational and social problems . . . [Princeton, Princeton university press, 1918] 3 p. l., 42 p.

University of Chicago, 1917, PH. D.
"Private edition distributed by the University of Chicago libraries, Chicago, Illinois."
"Reprinted from the Psychological monographs, vol. XXV, whole
no. 110, 1918."
19–1278   BF321.F85

107 **Fulmer, Henry Luman,** 1888–
Influence of carbonates of magnesium and calcium on
bacteria of certain Wisconsin soils . . . Washington,
Govt. print. off., 1918. cover-title, p. 463–504.

University of Wisconsin, 1917, PH. D.
Thesis note stamped on cover.
"Reprinted from Journal of agricultural research, vol. XII, no.
8 . . . February 25, 1918."
18–15674   QR111.F8

108 **Fundenburg, George Baer,** 1893–
Feudal France in the French epic, a study of feudal
French institutions in history and poetry . . . Prince-
ton, N. J., 1918. 4 p. l., 121 p.

Columbia university, 1919, PH. D.
20–5147   PQ155.F5F8

109 **Furman, Nathaniel Howell,** 1892–
The use of hydrofluoric acid in analysis and The
behavior of solutions of stannic fluoride . . . [Easton,
Pa., Eschenbach printing co., 1918] 23 p.

Princeton university, 1917, PH. D.
18–20628   QD181.F1F8

110 **Gaehr, Paul Frederick,** 1880–

The specific heat of tungsten at incandescent temperatures . . .   Lancaster, Pa., Press of the. New era printing company [1918]   [1], [396]–423 p.

Cornell university, 1918, PH. D.
"Reprinted from the Physical review, vol. XII, no. 5, November, 1918."
19–7024   QC295.G25

111 **Gallaher, Ruth Augusta,** 1882–

Legal and political status of women in Iowa, an historical account of the rights of women in Iowa from 1838 to 1918 . . .   Iowa City, Ia., 1918.   xii, 300 p.

University of Iowa, 1918, PH. D.
19–4624   HQ1256.I8G3

112 **Gardner, Max William,** 1890–

. . . Anthracnose of cucurbits . . .   Washington, Govt. print. off., 1918.   cover-title, 68 p.

(U. S. Dept. of agriculture. Bulletin no. 727. Professional paper)
University of Wisconsin, 1917, PH. D.
Thesis note stamped on cover.
Agr 19–9   SB741.A55G3

113 **Garretson, William Van Nest,** 1879–

On the asymptotic solution of the non-homogeneous linear differential equation of the n-th order.   A particular solution . . .   [Baltimore, 1918]   1 p. l., p. [341]–350.

University of Michigan, 1916, PH. D.
"Reprinted from American journal of mathematics, vol. XL, no. 4, October, 1918."
19–3249   QA377.G3

114 **Garrett, Mitchell Bennett,** 1881–

The French colonial question 1789–1791; dealings of the Constituent assembly with problems arising from the revolution in the West Indies . . .   Ann Arbor, Mich., G. Wahr [1918]   iv p., 1 l., 167 p.

Cornell university, 1910, PH. D.
Published in 1916 without thesis note.
19–7335   F1923.G234

115 **Garth, Thomas Russell**, 1872–
Mental fatigue during continuous exercise of a single
function . . . [New York] 1918. ix, 85 p., 1 l.

Columbia university, 1918, PH. D.
Published also as Columbia university contributions to philosophy
and psychology, vol. XXVI, no. 2 (Archives of psychology, no. 41)
19–16640   BF481.G3

116 **Giddings, Nahum James**, 1883–
. . . Infection and immunity in apple rust . . .
[Morgantown, W. Va., 1918] 71 p.

(West Virginia university agricultural experiment station . . .
Bulletin 170, December, 1918)
University of Wisconsin, 1918, PH. D.
Thesis note stamped on t.-p.
       S127.E52 no. 170

117 **Goad, Caroline Mabel.**
. . . Horace in the English literature of the
eighteenth century . . . New Haven, Yale university
press; [etc., etc.] 1918. vi p., 1 l., 641 p.

(Yale studies in English, A. S. Cook, editor. LVIII)
Yale university, 1916, PH. D.
18–20051   PA

118 **Good, Harry Gehman**, 1880–
. . . Benjamin Rush and his services to American
education . . . Berne, Ind., Witness press [1918]
x, 283 p.

University of Pennsylvania, 1915, PH. D.
Published also without thesis note.
18–9977   R154.R9G62

119 **Gordon, Newell Trimble**, 1891–
Potential measurements on the copper-nickel series of
alloys and some observations on brasses . . . Easton,
Pa., Eschenbach printing company, 1918. cover-title,
24 p.

Princeton university, 1919, PH. D.
19–17823   QD561.G65

120 **Goudge, Mabel Ensworth**, 1885–
A qualitative and quantitative study of Weber's
illusion . . . [Worcester, Mass., 1918] 1 p. l., p. 81–119.

Cornell university, 1914, PH. D.
"Reprinted from the American journal of psychology, January,
1918, vol. XXIX."
18–7765   QP451.G7

121 **Gowin, Enoch Burton,** 1883–
The selection and training of the business executive
. . . New York, The Macmillan company, 1918.
xii p., 1 l., 225 p.

Columbia university, 1918, PH. D.
18–17623   HF5500.G75

122 **Grant, Elmer Daniel,** 1873–
. . . Motion of a flexible cable in a vertical plane . . .
[Lancaster, Pa., Press of the New era printing company]
1918. 1 p. l., 28 p.

University of Chicago, 1916, PH. D.
"Private edition, distributed by the University of Chicago libraries, Chicago, Illinois."
18–20895   QA863.G7

123 **Greene, William Chase.**
Plato's view of poetry . . .

(*In* Harvard studies in classical philology. Cambridge, 1918.
vol. XXIX, p. 1–75)
"This essay in its original Latin form, entitled Quid de poetis
Plato censuerit, was presented in 1917 in partial fulfilment of the
requirements for the degree of doctor of philosophy in Harvard
university."
19–17336   PA25.H3   vol. XXIX

124 **Greenfield, Kent Roberts,** 1893–
Sumptuary law in Nürnberg; a study in paternal government . . . Baltimore, 1918. v, 7–140 p.

Johns Hopkins university, 1915, PH. D.
Published also as Johns Hopkins university studies in historical
and political science. ser. XXXVI, no. 2.
18–11716   DD901.N94G8

125 **Grout, Frank Fitch,** 1880–
The Duluth gabbro and its associated formations . . .
[New Haven? 1918] 6 pt. in 1 v.

Yale university, 1917, PH. D.
"A set of articles arranged for publication from a dissertation."
[pt. 1] Economic geology, vol. XIII, no. 3, May, 1918—[pt. 2]
American journal of science, vol. XLVI, Sept., 1918—[pt. 3] Journal
of geology, vol. XXVI, no. 5, July–August, 1918—[pt. 4] Journal of
geology, vol. XXVI, no. 6, Sept.–Oct., 1918—[pt. 5] Journal of geology,
vol. XXVI, no. 7, Oct.–Nov., 1918—[pt. 6] Journal of geology, vol.
XXVI, no. 7, Oct.–Nov., 1918.
20–3168   QE461.G88

126 **Hale, Robert Lee,** 1884–

Valuation and rate-making; the conflicting theories of the Wisconsin railroad commission, 1905–1917, with a chapter on the uncertainty of the United States Supreme court decisions, and a concluding chapter on the need of a revised principle of utility valuation . . . New York, 1918. 1 p. l., 5–157 p.

Columbia university, 1918, PH. D.
Published also as Studies in history, economics and public law, ed. by the Faculty of political science of Columbia university, vol. LXXX, no. 1, whole no. 185.
18–23261   HE1075.W8H32

127 **Hamer, Philip May.**

. . . The secession movement in South Carolina, 1847–1852 . . . Allentown, Pa., H. R. Haas & co., 1918. v, 152 p.

University of Pennsylvania, 1918, PH. D.
19–136   F273.H19

128 **Hamilton, Arthur,** 1886–

Sources of the religious element in Flaubert's Salammbô . . . Baltimore, The Johns Hopkins press, 1918. 1 p. l., 32 p., 1 l.

Johns Hopkins university, 1914, PH. D.
"An incomplete reprint from the Elliott monographs, no. 4."
18–23390   PQ2246.S4H32

129 **Hanke, Milton Theodore.**

. . . The oxidation of maltose in alkaline solution by hydrogen peroxide and by air, the preparation and study of maltobionic acid . . . Chicago, Ill., 1918. 3 p. l., 36 p.

University of Chicago, 1917, PH. D.
"Private edition, distributed by the University of Chicago libraries."
18–9973   QD321.H3

130 **Harding, Earle Atherton,** 1887–

A study of the occlusion of hydrogen and oxygen by metal electrodes . . . Easton, Pa., Eschenbach printing co., 1918. 2 p. l., [3]–26 p.

Princeton university, 1918, PH. D.
19–1720   QD571.H3

131 **Haring, Clarence Henry.**

Trade and navigation between Spain and the Indies in the time of the Hapsburgs . . . Cambridge, Harvard university press; [etc., etc.] 1918. xxviii, 371, [1] p.

(*Half-title:* Harvard economic studies . . . vol. xix)
Harvard university, 1916, PH. D.
Without thesis note.
"Part of the material in chapter vii was embodied in an article printed in the Quarterly journal of economics, in May, 1915, and the second half of chapter viii is largely an adaptation of another article, 'España y el Canal de Panamá,' which appeared in Hispania (London) in December 1912."—Pref.
18–8123   HF3685.H3

132 **Harvey, Rodney Beecher,** 1890–

. . . Hardening process in plants and developments from frost injury . . . [Washington, 1918] 1 p. l., p. 83–112.

University of Chicago, 1918, PH, D.
"Private edition, distributed by the University of Chicago libraries Chicago, Illinois."
"Reprinted from the Journal of agricultural research, vol. xv, no. 2, October 1918."
19–4926   QK756.H3

133 **Harvitt, Hélène Josephine,** 1884–

Eustorg de Beaulieu, a disciple of Marot, 1495 (?)– 1552 . . . Lancaster, Pa., Press of the New era printing company, 1918. ix, 164 p.

Columbia university, 1913, PH. D.
"Reprinted from the Romanic review, vol. v, no. 3 (1914), pp. 252–275; vol. vi, no. 1 (1915), pp. 42–59; no. 2, pp. 206–218; no. 3, pp. 298–326; vol. vii, no. 1 (1916), pp. 83–109; vol. ix, no. 3 (1918), pp. 319–344."
19–15144   PQ1605.B3H3

134 **Haseman, Mary Gertrude,** 1889–

On knots, with a census of the amphicheirals with twelve crossings . . . .Edinburgh, Printed by Neill & co., limited, 1918. 1 p. l., p. [235]–255.

Bryn Mawr college, 1918, PH. D.
"Reprinted from the Transactions of the Royal society of Edinburgh, vol. III, 1917."
18–22189   QA581.H3

135 **Hawley, Ira Myron,** 1884–

Insects injurious to the hop in New York, with special reference to the hop grub and the hop redbug . . . [Ithaca, N. Y., 1918] 1 p. l., p. 143–224.

Cornell university, 1916, PH. D.
Published as Cornell university agricultural experiment station Memoir 15, November, 1918.
19–7026   SB608.H8H3

136 **Hays, Heber Michel.**

. . . Notes on the Works and days of Hesiod, with introduction and appendix . . . Chicago, Ill., 1918. 2 p. l., 226 p.

University of Chicago, 1915, PH. D.
"Private edition, distributed by the University of Chicago libraries."
19–9294   PA4009.O7H3

137 **Hayward, Percy Roy.**

. . . Compensation for injuries to Canadian workmen . . . Toronto, Canada, Canada law book co., 1918 1 p. l., p. [281]–335.

University of Pennsylvania, 1918, PH. D.
Reprinted from Canada law journal, v. 54, nos. 8–9, August-September, 1918.
19–674   HD7816.C2H2

138 **Hebbert, Clarence Mark,** 1890—

Some circular curves generated by pencils of stelloids and their polars . . . [Urbana, 1918] 2 p. l., 14 p., 1 l.

University of Illinois, 1917, PH. D.
"Extracted from the Tôhoku mathematical journal, vol. 13, 1918, edited by Tsuruichi Hayashi."
18–19475   QA603.H45

139 **Heider, Andrew Bernard,** 1880–

The blessed Virgin Mary in early Christian Latin poetry . . . Washington, D. C., 1918. 79, [1] p.

Catholic university of America, 1918, PH. D.
19–2205   BT609.H4

140 **Henderson, Lawrence Melvin.**
    . . . The ratio of mesothorium to thorium . . .
[New York, 1918] 13 p.

University of Chicago, 1916, PH. D.

"Private edition, distributed by the University of Chicago libraries, Chicago, Illinois."

"Reprinted from the Journal of the American chemical society, vol. XL, no. 9, September, 1918."

19–3248   QC721.H4

141 **Henderson, Martin Perry.**
    . . . The black-leg disease of cabbage caused by *Phoma lingam* (Tode) Desmaz . . .

(*In* Phytopathology, official organ of the American phytopathological society. Baltimore, 1918. v. 8, no. 8, p. [379]–431)

University of Wisconsin, 1914, PH. D.

Thesis note stamp added to caption title, p. [379] and also on cover.

                                        SB741.B5H4

142 **Henderson, Walter Brooks Drayton.**

Swinburne and Landor, a study of their spiritual relationship and its effect on Swinburne's moral and poetic development . . . London, Macmillan and co., limited, 1918. viii, 304 p.

"The better part of this essay, together with its appendices, was submitted to the Faculty of Princeton university in partial fulfilment of the requirement for the degree of doctor of philosophy in English literature, in 1915."—Pref.

19–26021   PR5513.H4

143 **Hess, Raymond Washington.**

The scale of influence of substituents in paraffine monobasic acids. The divalent oxygen atom . . .
Easton, Pa., Eschenbach printing company, 1918.
26 p., 1 l.

University of Illinois, 1916, PH. D.

18–27261   QD305.A2H64

144 **Hewitt, Theodore Brown.**

Paul Gerhardt as a hymn writer and his influence on English hymnody . . . New Haven, Yale university press; [etc., etc.] 1918. xiv p., 1 l., 169 p.

"Presented to the Faculty of the Graduate school of Yale university in candidacy for the degree of doctor of philosophy in June, 1917."—Pref.

18–10288   BV330.G4H4

145 **Hicks, John Frederick Gross,** 1884–
The preparation and properties of yttrium mixed
metal . . . [Easton, Pa., 1918] 9, [1] p., 1 l.

University of Illinois, 1918, PH. D.
"Reprinted from the Journal of the American chemical society,
vol. XL, no. 11, page 1619."
19–13239 QD181.Y7H5

146 **Higby, Chester Penn,** 1885–
The religious policy of the Bavarian government
during the Napoleonic period . . . New York, 1918.
1 p. l., 5–347 p.

Columbia university, 1919, PH. D.
Published also as Studies in history, economics and public law,
ed. by the Faculty of political science of Columbia university, vol.
LXXXV, no. 1, whole no. 196.
19–12577 DD801.B381H5

147 **Higley, Ruth,** 1885–
Morphology and biology of some *Turbellaria* from the
Mississippi basin . . . [Urbana, 1918] 1 p. l., [5]–94
p.; 1 l.

University of Illinois, 1917, PH. D.
Published also as Illinois biological monographs, vol. IV, no. 3,
January, 1918.
"Contributions from the Zoological laboratory of the University
of Illinois under the direction of Henry B. Ward, no. 112."
20–1602 QL391.T9H6 1918a

148 **Hills, Thomas Lawrence,** 1890–
Influence of nitrates on nitrogen-assimilating bacteria . . . Washington, Govt. print. off., 1918. cover-
title, p. 183–230.

University of Wisconsin, 1917, PH. D.
Thesis note stamped on cover; also found in foot-note on p. 183.
"Reprinted from Journal of agricultural research, vol. XII, no. 4
. . . January 28, 1918."
18–18896 S651.H6

149 **Hixson, Arthur Warren,** 1880–
A study of the conditions essential for the commercial
manufacture of carvacrol . . . New York city, 1918.
2 p. l., 27 [1] p.

Columbia university, 1918, PH. D.
19–6704 RS431.C3H6

150 **Hoashi, Riichiro.**
. . . The problem of omnipotence in current theology . . . Chicago, Ill., 1918. 2 p. l., 113 p.
University of Chicago, 1917, PH. D.
"Private edition, distributed by the University of Chicago libraries."
18–20872   BT133.H6

151 **Hobson, Elsie Garland.**
. . . Educational legislation and administration in the
state of New York, 1777–1850 . . . Chicago, Ill., 1918.
5 p. l., 267 p.
University of Chicago, 1916, PH. D.
"Private edition, distributed by the University of Chicago libraries."
Published also as Supplementary educational monographs, pub. in
conjunction with the School review and the Elementary school journal,
vol. III, no. 1, whole no. 11.
19–670   LB2529.N75H6

152 **Hollingsworth, William Wiley.**
. . . Woodrow Wilson's political ideals as interpreted
from his works . . . Princeton, Princeton university
press, 1918. vi, 53 p.
University of Pennsylvania, 1918, PH. D.
18–19395   E767.H74

153 **Holtzhausser, Clara A.**
. . . An epigraphic commentary on Suetonius's life of
Tiberius . . . Philadelphia, Pa., 1918. 47 p.
University of Pennsylvania, 1918, PH. D.
19–8176   PA

154 **Hotz, Henry Gustave,** 1880–
First year algebra scales . . . New York city,
Teachers college, Columbia university, 1918. 3 p. l.,
87, [1] p.
Columbia university, 1918, PH. D.
18–18201   QA159.H7

155 **House, Roy Temple,** 1878–   *ed.*
. . . L'Ordene de chevalerie; an old French poem,
text, with introduction and notes . . . by Roy Temple
House . . . Chicago, Ill., 1918. 2 p. l., 69 p.
University of Chicago, 1917, PH. D.
"Private edition, distributed by the University of Chicago li-
braries."
19–9295   PQ1499.O38 1918

156 **Howell, Roger,** 1895–
The privileges and immunities of state citizenship . . .
Baltimore, 1918. vii, 9–121 p.

Johns Hopkins university, 1917, PH. D.
Published also as Johns Hopkins university studies in historical and
political science, ser. XXXVI, no. 3.
18–15115　　　　　　　　　　　　　　　　　　JK1756.H82

157 **Huang, Han Liang,** 1893–
The land tax in China . . . New York, 1918.
2 p. l., 7–181 p.

Columbia university, 1918, PH. D.
Published also as Studies in history, economics and public law,
ed. by the Faculty of political science of Columbia university. vol.
LXXX, no. 3; whole no. 187.
18–20900　　　　　　　　　　　　　　　　　　HJ4398.H82

158 **Huber, Harry Lee.**
. . . The pharmacology and toxicology of copper
salts of amino acids . . . [Baltimore, 1918] 1 p. l.,
p. 303–329.

University of Chicago, 1917, PH. D.
"Private edition, distributed by the University of Chicago libraries, Chicago, Illinois."
"Reprinted from the Journal of pharmacology and experimental
therapeutics, vol. XI, no. 4, May, 1918."
18–23721　　　　　　　　　　　　　　　　　　QP913.C9H8

159 **Hughes, Josiah Simpson,** 1884–
. . . Some nutritive properties of corn . . . Topeka, Kansas state printing plant, W. R. Smith, state
printer, 1918. cover-title, 3–39 p.

(Agricultural experiment station, Kansas state agricultural
college. Technical bulletin no. 5)
Ohio state university, 1917, PH. D.
Thesis note is a foot-note on p. 5.
19–4797　　　　　　　　　　　　　　　　　　S63.E45　no. 5

160 **Ide, Gladys Genevra.**
. . . The Witmer formboard and cylinders as tests
for children two to six years of age . . . Philadelphia,
Pa., The Psychological clinic press, 1918. 2 p. l., 24 p.

University of Pennsylvania, 1918, PH. D.
"Reprinted from the Psychological clinic, vol. XII, no. 3, May 15,
1918."
18–19386　　　　　　　　　　　　　　　　　　BF431.I3

161 **Jacob, Cary Franklin**, 1885–

The foundations and nature of verse . . . New York, Columbia university press, 1918. ix p., 1 l., 231 p., 1 l.

University of Virginia, 1917, PH. D.
Published also without thesis note.
20–5062   PE1505.J32

162 **Job, Thesle Theodore.**

Lymphatico-venous communications in the common rat and their significance . . . [Baltimore, 1918] cover-title, p. 467–491.

University of Iowa, 1917, PH. D.
Without thesis note.
"Author's abstract of this paper issued by the [Wistar institute] Bibliographic service, August 15."
"Reprinted from the American journal of anatomy, vol. 24, no. 4, November, 1918."
19–8253   QP115.J6

163 **Johnson, Franklin**, 1875–

The development of state legislation concerning the free negro . . . New York, 1918. vi, 207, [1] p.

Columbia university, 1918, PH. D.
Published in 1919 without thesis note.
19–16316   E185.6.J673

164 **Jones, Paul Van Brunt.**

. . . The household of a Tudor nobleman . . . Cedar Rapids, Ia., The Torch press, 1918. 5 p. l., 9–277 p.

University of Pennsylvania, 1912, PH. D.
"Reprinted from the University of Illinois studies in social sciences, volume VI, number 4."
18–18898   DA320.J7

165 **Kahn, Lina**, 1887–

Metaphysics of the supernatural as illustrated by Descartes . . . New York, Columbia university press, 1918. viii, 65, [1] p., 1 l.

Columbia university, 1916, PH. D.
Published also as Archives of philosophy, no. 9.
18–9795   .   B1878.S8K3   1918

166 **Kahn, Reuben Leon.**
Complement fixation with protein. substances . . .
[Baltimore, 1918]   1 p. l., 17 p.

New York university, 1916, D. SC.
"Reprinted from the Journal of immunology, vol. III, no. 4,
July, 1918."
19–4925   QR185.K3

167 **Kelly, Caleb Guyer,** 1887–
French Protestantism, 1559–1562 . . . Baltimore,
1918.   viii, 9–186 p.

Johns Hopkins university, 1916, PH. D.
Published also as Johns Hopkins university studies in history and
political science, series XXXVI, no. 4.
19–98   BR370.K32

168 **Kendall, John Norman,** 1891–
Abscission of flowers and fruits in the *Solanaceae*,
with special reference to *Nicotiana* . . . [Berkeley,
1918]   cover-title, p. [347]–428.

University of California, 1917, PH. D.
University of California publications in botany, v. 5, no. 12,
March 6, 1918, with a special thesis t.-p. dated May, 1917, attached
to the cover-title.
18–23722   QK763.K3

169 **Kenney, Arthur Webster,** 1891–
I. The equation of state of liquid ether. II. The
technical preparation of perchloric acid from potassium
perchlorate . . . [Cambridge, Mass.] Technology press,
1918.   18 p.
Massachusetts institute of technology, 1918, PH. D.
Abstract of thesis.
19–20159   QC307.K4

170 **Kent, Raymond Asa,** 1883–
A study of state aid to public schools in Minnesota . . . [Minneapolis] 1918.   ix, 183, [1] p.
Columbia university, 1917, PH. D.
Published also as University of Minnesota Studies in the social
sciences no. 11.
18–15790   LB2825.K42

171 **Kephart, Adam Perry,** 1883–

. . . Clinical studies of failures with the Witmer formboard . . . Philadelphia, The Psychological clinic press, 1918. 1 p. l., p. 229–253.

University of Pennsylvania, 1918, PH. D.
"Reprinted from the Psychological clinic, vol. XI, no. 8, January, 1918."
18–5472   LB1131.K4

172 **Kester, Roy Bernard,** 1882–

A study in valuation of the commercial balance sheet (comprising Chapters IV to XXVII inclusive of this volume) [Accounting theory and practice vol. II] . . . New York, The Ronald press company, 1918. xxiv, 796 p.

Columbia university, 1919, PH. D.
19–10377   HF5625.K353

173 **Keyes, Donald Babcock,** 1891–

Equilibria involving cyanogen iodide and the free energy of cyanogen . . . [Easton, Pa., 1918] cover-title, p. [472]–478.

University of California, 1917, PH. D.
Thesis t.-p. attached to the cover of the reprint from the Journal of the American chemical society, vol. XL, no. 3, March 1918, by Gilbert N. Lewis and Donald B. Keyes.
18–17505   QD181.C15K4

174 **Kiesselbach, Theodore Alexander.**

Studies concerning the elimination of experimental error in comparative crop tests . . . [Lincoln? 1918] 95 p.

University of Nebraska,   , PH. D.
"Reprint from Nebraska agricultural experiment station Research bulletin no. 13."
20–4631   SB186.K5

175 **Knox, John Knox.**

. . . Geology of the serpentine belt coleraine sheet, Thetford-Black Lake mining district, Quebec . . . Chicago, Ill., 1918. 73 p.

University of Chicago, 1917, PH. D.
Private edition, distributed by the University of Chicago libraries.
19–12686   QE193.K7

176 **Koller, Armin Hajman.**

   . . . The theory of environment, an outline of the history of the idea of milieu, and its present status. pt. I . . . Menasha, Wis., George Banta publishing company, 1918. 6 p. l., 104 p.

    University of Chicago, 1911, PH. D.
    Published also without thesis note.
    19–12075   GF51.K76

177 **Kraeling, Emil Gottlieb Heinrich,** 1892–

   . . . Aram and Israel; or, The Aramaeans in Syria and Mesopotamia . . . New York, Columbia university press, 1918. xvi, 155 p., 1 l.

    (Columbia university oriental studies, vol. XIII)
    Columbia university, 1917, PH. D.
    Published also without thesis note.
    18–10040   DS59.A7K82

178 **Kraus, Ezra Jacob,** 1885–

   Vegetation and reproduction with special reference to the tomato . . . by Ezra Jacob Kraus and Henry Reist Kraybill [Corvallis, Or., 1918] 2 p. l., 3–90 p.

    University of Chicago, 1917, PH. D.
    "This bulletin is the result of the cooperative efforts of Messrs. Kraus and Kraybill and has been submitted by them in fulfillment of the thesis requirements for the degree of doctor of philosophy from the University of Chicago."
    "Private edition, distributed by the University of Chicago libraries, Chicago, Illinois."
    "Reprinted from station bulletin 149, Oregon agricultural college, January, 1918."
    19–4629   SB349.K8

Kraybill, Henry Reist *see* 178 **Kraus, Ezra Jacob.**

179 **Kremers, Harry Cleveland.**

   Observations on the rare earths: the purification and atomic weight of dysprosium . . . [Urbana? 1918] 22 p., 1 l.

    University of Illinois, 1917, PH. D.
    18–27262   QD181.D8K8

180 **Kruse, Paul Jehu,** 1883–
The overlapping of attainments in certain sixth, seventh, and eighth grades . . . New York city, Teachers college, Columbia university, 1918. 3 p. l., 5–91, [1] p.
Columbia university, 1918, PH. D.
Published also as Contributions to education, Teachers college, Columbia university, no. 92.
19–4591   LB1131.K7

181 **Lamprecht, Sterling Power,** 1890–
The moral and political philosophy of John Locke . . .
New York, Columbia university press, 1918. viii, 168 p., 1 l.
Columbia university, 1918, PH. D.
"Reprinted from Archives of philosophy, no. 11."
19–654   B1297.L32

182 **Larsell, Olof,** 1886–
Studies on the nervus terminalis: mammals . . .
[Philadelphia, 1918] 68 p.
Northwestern university, 1918, PH. D.
"Reprinted from the Journal of comparative neurology, vol. 30, no. 1, December, 1918."
"Author's abstract of this paper issued by the [Wistar institute] Bibliographic service, December 9."
19–9535   QL939.L3

183 **Layng, Thomas Ernest.**
Low temperature carbonization of coal and a study of the resulting tars . . . [Urbana? 1918] 34, [2] p.
University of Illinois, 1915, PH. D.
18–17017   PT953.L3

184 **Le Duc, Alma de Lande,** 1878–
Gontier Col and the French pre-renaissance . . .
New York, 1918. vii, 103, [1] p.
Columbia university, 1916, PH. D.
"Reprinted from the Romanic review, vol. VII, no. 4, 414–457, 1916; vol. VIII, no. 2, 145–165, and no. 3, 290–306, 1917."
19–9562   PQ1559.C56L4

185 **Lefferts, Walter,** 1875–
. . . Tidewater Maryland, an embayed coast plain . . . Philadelphia, International printing company, 1918. 64 p.
University of Pennsylvania, 1918, PH. D.
18–17020   HC107.M3L4

186 Leffingwell, Georgia Williams, 1893–

Social and private life at Rome in the time of Plautus
and Terence . . .   New York, 1918.   2 p. l., 7–141 p.

Columbia university, 1918, PH. D.

Published also as Studies in history, economics and public law,
edited by the Faculty of political science of Columbia university.
vol. LXXXI, no. 1; whole no. 188.

19–513   DG78.L42

187 Leman, Edwin Daniel.

. . . The relation between the alpha-ray activities
and ranges of radioactive substances . . .   Chicago,
Ill., 1918.   2 p. l., 20 p.

University of Chicago, 1915, PH. D.

"Private edition, distributed by the University of Chicago libraries."

18–14654   QC721.L5

188 Levi, Gerson Benedict.

Gnomic literature in Bible and Apocrypha, with
special reference to tbe gnomic fragments and their
bearing on the proverb collections . . .   [Philadephia?
1918]   1 p. l., 7–113 p.

University of Pennsylvania, 1910, PH. D.

20–4628   BS1455.L4

189 Lindstrom, Ernest Walter, 1891–

Chlorophyll inheritance in maize . . .   [Ithaca, 1918]
68 p.

Cornell university, 1918, PH. D.

"Reprint from the Cornell university experiment station Memoir
13, August 1918."

"Paper no. 65, Department of plant breeding, Cornell university,
Ithaca, New York."

19–16518   QK981.L5 1918a

190 Lockert, Charles Lacy, 1888–   *ed.*

The fatal dowry, by Philip Massinger and Nathaniel
Field, ed., from the original quarto, with introduction
and notes . . . by Charles Lacy Lockert, jr. . . .   Lancaster, Pa., Press of the New era printing company,
1918.   iii, 167 p.

Princeton university, 1916, PH. D.

18–15776   PR2704.F5 1918

191 **Lonn, Ella.**

. . . Reconstruction in Louisiana after 1868 . . . New York and London, G. P. Putnam's sons, 1918. 1 p. l., 95 p.

University of Pennsylvania, 1911, PH. D.

Comprises the first four chapters of a much larger work which was published without thesis note but with the same title.

18–19396   F375.L84

192 **Lowe, Boutelle Ellsworth,** 1890–

International aspects of the labor problem . . . N[ew] Y[ork] W. D. Gray [1918]   2 p. l., 3–128 p., 1 l.

Columbia university, 1918, PH. D.

19–15539   HD4851.L6

193 **Lowrey, Lawrence Tyndale,** 1888–

Northern opinion of approaching secession, October, 1859–November, 1860 . . .   Northampton, Mass., 1918. 2 p. l., p. [191]–258.

Columbia university, 1917, PH. D.

"Reprinted from the Smith college studies in history, volume III, number 4."

18–20898   E436.L92

194 **Ludwig, Clinton Albert,** 1886–

The influence of illuminating gas and its constituents on certain bacteria and fungi . . .   Lancaster, Pa., Press of the New era printing company, 1918.   1 p. l., 31 p.

University of Michigan, 1917, PH. D.

"Reprinted from the American journal of botany, 5: 1–31, January, 1918."

"Publication no. 167 from the Botanical department of the University of Michigan."

18–7769   QK751.L7

195 **Lutz, Harley Leist,** 1882–

The state tax commission; a study of the development and results of state control over the assessment of property for taxation . . .   Awarded the David A. Wells prize for the year 1915–16, and pub. from the income of the David A. Wells fund.   Cambridge, Harvard university press; [etc., etc.] 1918.   ix, 673, [1] p.

(*Half-title:* Harvard economic studies . . .   vol. XVII)

"Submitted as a doctoral dissertation at Harvard in 1914, and is now published after a thorough revision."—Pref.

18–3376   HJ3241.L8

196 **McCann, Mary Agnes,** *sister*, 1851–
Archbishop Purcell and the archdiocese of Cincinnati,
a study based on original sources . . . Washington,
D. C., 1918. 108 p.

197 **McClugage, Harry Bruce.**
Experiments on the utilization of nitrogen, calcium,
and magnesium in diets containing carrots and spinach,
by Harry B. McClugage and Lafayette B. Mendel . . .
[Baltimore, 1918]   cover-title, p. 353–366.

"The data in this paper are taken from the dissertation presented by
Harry B. McClugage for the degree of doctor of philosophy, Yale university, 1918."
"From the Sheffield laboratory of physiological chemistry, Yale
university, New Haven."
"Reprinted from the Journal of biological chemistry, vol. xxxv, no.
2, August, 1918."

198 **McCrosky, Carl Raymond,** 1890–
The oxidizing action of potassium dichromate as compared with that of pure iodine . . . Columbus, O.,
1918.   15 p.

199 **MacDaniels, Laurence Howland,** 1888–
The histology of the phloem in certain woody angiosperms . . . Ithaca, N. Y., 1918.   1 p. l., p. 347–378.

Cornell university, 1917, PH. D.
"Reprinted from the American journal of botany, 5 . . . July,
1918."

200 **McDougle, Ivan Eugene.**
Slavery in Kentucky, 1792–1865 . . . [Lancaster,
Pa., Press of the New era printing company, 1918]
2 p. l., 125 p.

Clark university, 1918, PH. D.
"Reprinted from the Journal of negro history, vol. iii, no. 3, July,
1918."

201 **McEwen, Robert Stanley,** 1888–

The reactions to light and to gravity in *Drosophila* and its mutants . . . [Baltimore, 1918] cover-title, 49–106 p., 1 l.

Columbia university, 1917, PH. D.

"Author's abstract of this paper issued by the [Wistar institute] Bibliographic service, December 22."

"Reprinted from the Journal of experimental zoölogy, vol. 25, no. 1, February, 1918."

18–13248   QH650.M3

202 **McWhorter, Golder Louis,** 1888–

Some clinical and experimental observations on gastric acidity use of the gas-chain method . . . [Philadelphia, etc., 1918] cover-title, 13 p.

University of Minnesota, 1918, PH. D.

Slip with thesis note mounted on p. 2 of cover.

"From the American journal of the medical sciences, May, 1918, no. 5, vol. CLV, p. 672."

18–23455   QP193.M3

203 **Maddox, William Arthur,** 1883–

The free school idea in Virginia before the civil war, a phase of political and social evolution . . . New York city, Teachers college, Columbia university, 1918. vi p., 1 l., 225 p., 1 l.

Columbia university, 1918, PH. D.

Published also as Contributions to education, Teachers college, Columbia university, no. 93.

19–4102   LA379.M25

204 **Mahood, Samuel Arthur,** 1884–

Tetraiodophenolphthalein and tetraiodophenoltetrachlorophthalein and some of their derivatives, by W. R. Orndorff and S. A. Mahood . . . [Easton, Pa., 1918] 1 p. l., p. [937]–955.

"A reprint of an article based upon a thesis submitted to the Faculty of the Graduate school of Cornell university for the degree of doctor of philosophy, by Samuel Arthur Mahood." 1917.

W. R. Orndorff, instructor under whom thesis was written.

"Reprinted from the Journal of the American chemical society, vol. XL, no. 6, June, 1918."

19–7790   QD441 O8

205 **Marcus, Joseph K.**, 1894–
The synthesis of mono-amino-flavones, of flavone-azo-beta-naphthol dyes and of other flavone derivatives
. . . New York, Chauncey Holt company [1918] 38 p.
Columbia university, 1918, PH. D.
19–10022   QD441.M2

206 **Martin, Asa Earl**, 1885–
The anti-slavery movement in Kentucky prior to 1850
. . . [Louisville? Ky., 1918] 165 p.
Cornell university, 1915, PH. D.
Published also as Filson club publication no. 29.
19–8009   E445.K3M39

207 **Marvin, Donald Mitchell.**
. . . Occupational propinquity as a factor in marriage selection . . . [Philadelphia?] 1918. 22 p.
University of Pennsylvania, 1918, PH. D.
19–675   HQ728.M3

208 **Mateer, Florence.**
Child behavior; a critical and experimental study of young children by the method of conditioned reflexes
. . . Boston, R. G. Badger [1918] 2 p. l., 7–239 p.
Clark university, 1916, PH. D.
Published also without thesis note.
18–5323   LB1121.M272

209 **Mayer, Eli**, 1880–
. . . War and religion; a sociological study . . .
Philadelphia, Pa., 1918. 100 p.
University of Pennsylvania, 1918, PH. D.
18–12850   BL65.W2M3

210 **Mead, Arthur Raymond, 1880–**
The development of free schools in the United States as illustrated by Connecticut and Michigan . . . New York city, Teachers college, Columbia university, 1918.
3 p. l., v–xi, 236 p., 1 l.
Columbia university, 1918, PH. D.
Published also as Contributions to education, Teachers college, Columbia university, no. 91.
19–4103   LA249.M4

211 **Messer, William Stuart,** 1882–
The dream in Homer and Greek tragedy . . . New York, Columbia university press, 1918. viii p., 1 l., 105, [1] p.

(*Half-title:* Columbia university studies in classical philology)
Columbia university, 1918, PH. D.
Published also without thesis note.
18–15775   PA

212 **Michel, Virgil G.,** 1890–
The critical principles of Orestes A. Brownson . . . Washington, D. C., 1918. 106 p., 1 l.

Catholic university of America,   , PH. D.
19–2947   PS1145.B7Z7

213 **Miller, Edward Alanson,** 1866–
. . . The history of educational legislation in Ohio from 1803 to 1850 . . . [Columbus, 1918] 1 p. l., 286 p.

University of Chicago, 1915, PH. D.
"Private edition distributed by the University of Chicago libraries, Chicago, Illinois."
"Reprinted from Ohio archaeological and historical quarterly, volume XXVII, nos. 1 and 2, January and April, 1918."
18–20535   LA346.M6

214 **Minnick, John Harrison,** 1877–
. . . An investigation of certain abilities fundamental to the study of geometry . . . Lancaster, Pa., Press of the New era printing company, 1918. vii, 108 p.

University of Pennsylvania, 1918, PH. D.
18–5516   QA461.M7

215 **Mohler, Fred Loomis,** 1893–
Resonance radiation of sodium vapor excited by one of the D lines . . . [Lancaster, Pa., 1918] 1 p. l., [70]–80, [1] p.

Johns Hopkins university, 1917, PH. D.
"Reprinted from the Physical review, n. s., vol. XI, no. 1, January, 1918."
18–7763   QC462.S6M6

216 **Mohlman, Floyd William.**
The activated-sludge method of sewage treatment . . . [Urbana? 1918] 43, [1] p.

University of Illinois, 1916, PH. D.
18–27259   TD765.M6

217 **Moley, Raymond,** 1886–
The state movement for efficiency and economy . .
[New York? 1918]   2 p. l., iii–vi, 165 p.
Columbia university, 1918, PH. D.
18–17492   JK2443.M7

218 **Moore, Charlotte.**
. . . The dramatic works of Thomas Nabbes . . .
Part I.   Menasha, Wis., George Banta publishing company, 1918.   3 p. l., 61, [1] p.
University of Pennsylvania, 1915, PH. D.
"Part II of this thesis consists of a transcript of the quarto text, 1637,
of Hannibal and Scipio, with some introductory pages remaining from
the part here published.   The text is accompanied with notes and a
glossary."
18–22114   PR2719.N3Z7

219 **Moral, José D.,** 1885–
The action of certain antiseptics, toxic salts, and alkaloids on the bacteria and protozoa of the intestine of
the rabbit . . .   [New York? 1918]   12 p.
Columbia university, 1918, PH. D.
20–10246   RM647.M6

220 **Morimoto, Kokichi,** 1879–
The standard of living in Japan . . . Baltimore,
1918.   vii, 9–147 p., 1 l.
Johns Hopkins university, 1916, PH. D.
Published also as Johns Hopkins university studies in historical
and political science . . . ser. XXXVI, no. 1.
18–2748   HD7057.M7   1918a

221 **Morris, Harold Hulett.**
. . . A study of the chemistry of gold at high temperatures and pressures . . .   [Easton, Pa., 1918]   cover-
title, p. [917]–927.
University of Wisconsin, 1917, PH. D.
Thesis note is a foot-note on p. [917]; also stamped on cover.
"Reprinted from the Journal of the American chemical society,
vol. XL, no. 6.   June, 1918."
18–15670   QD181.A9M8

222 **Mortimer, Franklin Spencer,** 1891–

The electromotive force and free energy of dilution of lithium chloride in aqueous and alcoholic solutions . . . Easton, Pa., Eschenbach printing company, 1918.   19, [1] p.

University of Iowa, 1917, PH. D.
19–7020   QD561.M85

223 **Mullinix, Raymond David.**

. . .   I. The conductivity of alkaline earth formates in anhydrous formic acid.   II. The manufacture of potassium manganate . . .   Chicago, Ill., 1918.   13 p.

University of Chicago, 1918, PH. D.
"Private edition, distributed by the University of Chicago libraries."
19–16520   QD305.A2M97

224 **Munro, Dana Gardner.**

. . .   The five republics of Central America; their political and economic development and their relations with the United States . . .   New York [etc.]   Oxford university press, 1918.   viii p., 1 l., 332 p.

University of Pennsylvania, 1917, PH. D.
Published also by the Carnegie endowment for international peace, Division of economics and history.
18–7046   F1428.M952

225 **Musselman, John Rogers,** 1890–

The set of eight self-associated points in space . . . [Baltimore, 1918]   1 p. l., p. [69]–86, 1 l.

Johns Hopkins university, 1916, PH. D.
"Reprinted from American journal of mathematics, vol. XL, no. 1, January, 1918."
18–7768   QA603.M9

226 **Musser, John.**

. . .   The establishment of Maximilian's empire in Mexico . . .   Menasha, Wis., George Banta publishing company, 1918.   2 p. l., 100 p.

University of Pennsylvania, 1912, PH. D.
18–11153   F1233.M98

227 **Muttkowski, Richard Anthony,** 1887–
The fauna of Lake Mendota . . . [Madison, Wis.]
1918. cover-title, p. 374–482.

University of Wisconsin, 1916, PH. D.
Thesis note stamped on cover.
"Reprinted from the Transactions of the Wisconsin academy of
sciences, arts, and letters, vol. XIX, part I."
19–27366   QL146.M8

228 **Nagler, Floyd August,** 1892–
Verification of the Bazin weir formula by hydro-chemical gaugings . . . [New York, 1918] cover-title, p.
[3]–54.

University of Michigan, 1917, PH. D.
From the Proceedings of the American society of civil engineers,
vol. XLIV, no. 1. Papers and discussions.
18–7522   TC175.N3

229 **Nakahara, Waro.**
Studies of amitosis, its physiological relations in the
adipose cells of insects, and its probable significance . . .
Philadelphia [1918] 1 p. l., p. 483–525.

Cornell university, 1918, PH. D.
"Author's abstract of this paper issued by the [Wistar institute]
Bibliographic service, January 12."
"Reprinted from the Journal of morphology, vol. 30, no. 2, March,
1918."
18–15673   QH605.N2

230 **Nelson, Thurlow Christian.**
On the origin, nature, and function of the crystalline
style of lamellibranchs . . . [Boston, 1918] cover-
title, p. 53–111.

University of Wisconsin, 1917, PH. D.
Thesis note stamped on cover; also found in foot-note on p. 53.
"Author's abstract of this paper issued by the [Wistar institute]
Bibliographic service, April 20."
"Reprinted from Journal of morphology, vol. 31, no. 1, June,
1918."
20–3141   QL430.6.N4

231 **Newell, Anna Grace,** 1876–

The comparative morphology of the genitalia of insects . . . [Columbus, O., 1918] 2 p. l., p. 109–142.

University of Illinois, 1916, PH. D.

"Reprinted from the Annals of the Entomological society of America, vol. XI, no. 2, June, 1918."

"Contribution from the Entomological laboratories of the University of Illinois, no. 51."

19–14377 QL494.N4

232 **Noble, Stuart Grayson,** 1886–

Forty years of the public schools in Mississippi, with special reference to the education of the negro . . . New York city, Teachers college, Columbia university, 1918. iv p., 1 l., 142 p., 1 l.

Columbia university, 1918, PH. D.

Published also as Contributions to education, Teachers college, Columbia university, no. 94.

19–4104 LA313.N6

233 **Noel, Francis Regis,** 1891–

A history of the bankruptcy clause of the Constitution of the United States of America . . . [Gettysburg, Gettysburg compiler print, 1918] 210 p.

Catholic university of America, 1918, PH. D.

20–1136 HG3766.N6

234 **Norlie, Olaf Morgan,** 1876–

Principles of expressive reading, impression before expression . . . Boston, The Gorham press, 1918. 2 p. l., 3–190 p.

University of Minnesota, 1908, PH. D.

Thesis note is Note 1 on p. 165.

18–19505 PN4145.N6

235 **Northcott, Clarence Hunter,** 1880–

Australian social development . . . New York, 1918. 2 p. l., 7–303 p., 1 l.

Columbia university, 1918, PH. D.

Published also as Studies in history, economics and public law, ed. by the Faculty of political science of Columbia university, vol. LXXXI, no. 2; whole no. 189.

18–21106 HN843.N72

236 **Nourse, Edwin Griswold,** 1883–
    . . . The Chicago produce market; a study of market mechanism as a factor in price determination . . . Boston, Houghton Mifflin company, 1918.   6 p. l., 304 p., 1 l.

    (*Half-title:* Hart, Schaffner & Marx prize essays.   xxv)
    University of Chicago, 1915, PH. D.
    Published also without thesis note.
    18–15501   HD9008.C4N7 1918 a

237 **Paine, George Porter.**
    . . . Report on modes of air motion and the equations of the general circulation of the earth's atmosphere . . . Washington, Govt. print. off., 1918.   1 p. l., p. 311–323.

    University of Wisconsin, 1918, PH. D.
    Thesis note stamped on t.-p.
    "Reprinted from Monthly weather review, July, 1918, 46."
    20–2107   QC931.P3

238 **Parkins, Almon Ernest.**
    . . . The historical geography of Detroit . . .   Chicago, Ill., 1918.   xix, 356 p.

    University of Chicago, 1914, PH. D.
    "A private edition distributed by the University of Chicago libraries."
    "University series, III. The Michigan historical commission, Lansing, Michigan."
    18–14522   F574.D4P27

239 **Parr, Rosalie Mary.**
    The response of *Pilobolus* to light . . .   [London, 1918]   1 p. l., [177]–205 p., 1 l.

    University of Illinois, 1916, PH. D.
    "Reprint from the Annals of botany, vol. XXXII, no. CXXVI, April, 1918."
    19–8251   QK776.P3

240 **Paschal, Franklin Cressey,** 1890–
    . . . The Witmer cylinder test . . .   Hershey, Pa., The Hershey press, 1918.   54 p.

    University of Pennsylvania, 1918, PH. D.
    18–6790   LB1131.P3
    33564°—21——5

241 **Pasmore, Daniel Frederick,** 1889–

Karl Gutzkow's short stories, a study in the technique
of narration . . . [Urbana? 1918] 4 p. l., 122 p., 1 l.

University of Illinois, 1917, PH. D.
19–27040　　　　　　　　　　　　　　　　　　PT2282.Z6P3

242 **Paterson, Robert Gildersleeve.**

. . . Wage payment legislation in the United States
. . . [Washington, D. C.] 1918. 186 p.

University of Pennsylvania, 1909, PH. D.
Published also as Bulletin of the U. S. Bureau of labor statistics,
whole no. 229.
18–13888　　　　　　　　　　　　　　　　　　HD4935.U4P4

243 **Peck, Edward Bates.**

An investigation of the reaction between antimony
and solutions of sodium in liquid ammonia . . .
Easton, Pa., Eschenbach printing company [1918] 15 p.

Clark university, 1917, PH. D.
Reprinted from the Journal of the American chemical society,
vol. XL, no. 2, February, 1918, p. 335–347.
19–2853　　　　　　　　　　　　　　　　　　QD181.S3P4

244 **Perlman, Selig.**

Upheaval and reorganisation (since 1876) . . .

(*In* Commons, J. R. History of labour in the United States. New
York, 1918. vol. II, pt. 6, p. [193]–537)
University of Wisconsin, 1915, PH. D.
Without thesis note.

HD8066.C7

245 **Peters, Charles Clinton,** 1887–

. . . Selection and organization of materials for a
course in "the control of conduct" for secondary
schools . . . Spring City, Pa., The Interborough press
[1918] 120 p.

University of Pennsylvania, 1916, PH. D.
18–9902　　　　　　　　　　　　　　　　　　LC268.P4

246 **Phinney, Chester Squire, 1886–**

. . . Francis Lieber's influence on American thought
and some of his unpublished letters . . . Philadelphia.
International printing co., 1918. 85 p.

University of Pennsylvania, 1918, PH. D.
18–9808　　　　　　　　　　　　　　　　　　JC212.L8P5

247 **Pierce, William Dwight,** 1881–
Comparative morphology of the order *Strepsiptera*
together with records and descriptions of insects . . .
[Washington, D. C., 1918]   cover-title, 3 p. l., p. 391–501.

George Washington university, 1917, PH. D.
"No. 2242.—From the Proceedings of the United States National
museum, vol. 54."
20–5879   QL599.P5

248 **Pinney, Mary Edith,** 1881–
A study of the relation of the behavior of the chroma-
tin to development and heredity in teleost hybrids . . .
[Boston, 1918]   1 p. l., p. 225–291, 1 l.

Bryn Mawr college, 1918, PH. D.
"Author's abstract of this paper issued by the [Wistar institute]
Bibliographic service, August 7."
"Reprinted from the Journal of morphology, volume 31, number 2,
September, 1918."
18–22190   QH605.P4

249 **Pollock, Ivan Lester,** 1887–
History of economic legislation in Iowa . . .   Iowa
City, Ia., 1918.   vi p., 1 l., 386 p.

University of Iowa, 1917, PH. D.
Published also in Iowa economic history series.
19–4625   HC107.I8P7

250 **Porter, Kirk Harold.**
. . . A history of suffrage in the United States . . .
Chicago, Ill., The University of Chicago press, 1918.
2 p. l., vii–xi, 260 p.

University of Chicago, 1918, PH. D.
Published also without thesis note.
18–22991   JK1846.P82

251 **Powell, Fred Wilbur,** 1881–
The recent movement for state budget reform: 1911–
1917 . . .   [New York, 1918]   2 p. l., iii–ix, 157 p.

Columbia university, 1918, PH. D.
"Reprinted from Municipal research, New York, November, 1917,
no. 91."
18–12921   HJ2053.A1P7

252 **Pratt, Frank Randall,** 1876–

Heats of dilution and their variations with temperature . . . [Philadelphia] J. B. Lippincott company,
1918. cover-title, p. 663–695.

> Princeton university, 1917, PH. D.
> "Reprinted from the Journal of the Franklin institute, May, 1918."
> 18–14653   QC310.P8

253 **Price, Henry Ferris,** 1884–

. . . Fundamental regions for certain finite groups in
S_4 . . . [Baltimore, 1918] [1], [108]–112 p.

> University of Pennsylvania, 1915, PH. D.
> "Reprinted from American journal of mathematics, vol. XL, no. 1,
> January, 1918."
> 18–7757   QA171.P9

254 **Purcell, Richard Joseph.**

Connecticut in transition, 1775–1818 . . . Washington, American historical association; [etc., etc.] 1918.
x, 471 p.

> Yale university, 1916, PH. D.
> Without thesis note.
> "To this essay was awarded the Justin Winsor prize in American
> history for 1916."
> 19–3751   F99.P98

255 **Putnam, James William.**

. . . The Illinois and Michigan canal; a study in
economic history . . . Illinois centennial publication.
Chicago, The University of Chicago press, 1918. xiii,
213 p.

> (Chicago historical society's collection, vol. x)
> University of Wisconsin, 1909, PH. D.
> Thesis note stamped on t.-p.
> 18–8108   TC625.I2P8

256 **Quigley, Harold Scott.**

. . . The immunity of private property from capture
at sea . . . Madison, Wis., 1918. 200 p.

> (Bulletin of the University of Wisconsin, no. 918. Economics and
> political science series, v. 9, no. 2)
> University of Wisconsin, 1916, PH. D.
> 19–27367   H31.W63   vol. 9, no. 2

257 **Quimby, Mary Agnes.**
. . . The nature background in the dramas of Gerhart
Hauptmann . . . Philadelphia, International printing
company, 1918. 68 p.

University of Pennsylvania, 1918, PH. D.
20–17029   PT2616.Z9Q5

258 **Ramler, Otto Joseph,** 1887–
On the three-cusped hypocycloids fulfilling certain
assigned conditions . . . Washington, D. C., 1918.
iv, 22 p.

Catholic university of America, 1918, PH. D.
19–15474   QA623.R3

259 **Rathbun, Mary Jane,** 1860–
The grapsoid crabs of America . . . [Washington,
1918] cover-title, xxii, 461 p.

George Washington university, 1917, PH. D.
"Bulletin 97, U. S. National museum, January 25, 1918."
18–9972   QL444.D3R23 1918a

260 **Rawlins, Charles Henry,** 1889–
Complete systems of concomitants of the three-point
and the four-point in elementary geometry . . . [Balti-
more, 1918] · 1 p. l., [155]–173 p., 1 l.

Johns Hopkins university, 1916, PH. D.
"Reprinted from American journal of mathematics, vol. XL, no. 2,
April, 1918."
18–11524   QA603.R3

261 **Ray, Arthur Benning,** 1889–
The electrolysis of solutions of the rare earths . . .
[Easton, Pa., 1918] 10 p.

Cornell university, 1916, PH. D.
"Reprinted from the Journal of the American chemical society,
vol. XL, no. 1, January, 1918."
19–7786   QD172.R2R3

262 **Rees, Edwin Arthur.**
Heterogeneous equilibria between aqueous and metallic solutions. The interaction of mixed salt solutions
and liquid amalgams. A study of the ionization relations of potassium and strontium chlorides in mixtures
. . . [Easton, Pa., 1918] 2 p. l., 46 p., 1 l.

University of Illinois, 1918, PH. D.
"Reprinted from the Journal of the American chemical society,
vol. XL, no. 12, p. 1802."
19–13238   QD501.R4

263 **Rees, Maurice Holmes.**
. . . The influence of pituitary extracts on the daily output of urine . . . [Boston, 1918] 1 p. l., p. 471–484.
University of Chicago, 1917, PH. D.
"Private edition, distributed by the University of Chicago libraries, Chicago, Illinois."
"Reprinted from the American journal of physiology, vol. XLV, no. 4, March, 1918."
18–20627   QP211.R43

264 **Reuter, Edward Byron.**
. . . The mulatto in the United States, including a study of the rôle of mixed-blood races throughout the world . . . Boston, R. G. Badger, 1918. 1 p. l., 5–417 p.
University of Chicago, 1919, PH. D.
Published also without thesis note.
20–1443   E185.62.R45

265 **Ridgley, Frank Harris.**
Jewish ethical idealism . . . Boston, The Gorham press, 1918. 97 p.
University of Pennsylvania, 1916, PH. D.
Published also without thesis note in the Library of religious thought.
19–655   BM565.R52

266 **Robbins, Wilfred William.**
. . . Successions of vegetation in Boulder Park, Colorado . . . [Chicago, 1918] 1 p. l., p. 493–525.
University of Chicago, 1917, PH. D.
"Private edition, distributed by the University of Chicago libraries, Chicago, Illinois."
"Reprinted from the Botanical gazette, vol. LXV, no. 6; June, 1918."
"Contributions from the Hull botanical laboratory 238."
18–19479   QK941.C6R7

267 **Roberts, Elmer,** 1886–
Fluctuations in a Mendelian character and selection . . . Philadelphia, 1918. 1 p. l., 157–192 p., 1 l.
University of Illinois, 1917, PH. D.
"Author's abstract of this paper issued by the [Wistar institute] Bibliographic service October 8."
"Paper no. 7 from the Laboratory of genetics, Department of animal husbandry, University of Illinois."
"Reprinted from the Journal of experimental zoölogy, vol. 27, no. 2, November, 1918."
19–14376   QH431.R7

268 **Roberts, John William.**
. . . The sources of apple bitter-rot infections . . .
Washington [Govt. print. off.] 1918. 26 p.

(U. S. Dept. of agriculture. Bulletin no. 684. (Professional
paper))
George Washington university, 1917, PH. D.
. Thesis note stamped on p. 1.
Agr 18–772   SB741.A5R6

269 **Robinson, Charles Summers,** 1885–
Some experiments on the manifestation of osmotic
pressure with membranes of chemically inert materials
. . . [Ithaca, N. Y., 1918] cover-title, p. [99]–127,
[153]–183.

University of Michigan, 1917, PH. D.
Reprinted from two articles by S. L. Bigelow and C. S. Robinson
in the Journal of physical chemistry, vol. 22, 1918.
20–5886   QD543.R6

270 **Robinson, Mabel Louise.**
. . . The curriculum of the woman's college . . .
Washington, Govt. print. off., 1918. 140 p.

([U. S.] Bureau of education. Bulletin, 1918, no. 6)
Columbia university, 1916, PH. D.
Slip with thesis note pasted on t.-p.
E 18–827   LC1756.R72

271 **Rodebush, Worth Huff,** 1887–
The freezing points of concentrated solutions and the
free energy of solution of salts . . . [New York, 1918]
cover-title, p. [1204]–1213.

University of California, 1917, PH. D.
Reprint from the Journal of the American chemical society, vol.
XL, no. 8, August 1918, with a special thesis t.-p. dated May, 1917,
attached to the cover-title.
19–1719   QD545.R6

272 **Roesch,** *Sister* **Mary Jeanette,** 1884–
Vocational preparation of youth in Catholic schools
. . . Washington, D. C., 1918. 73 p.

Catholic university of America, 1918, PH. D.
19–2624   LC485.R6

273 **Rogers, Agnes Low,** 1884–

Experimental tests of mathematical ability and their prognostic value . . . New York city, Teachers college,. Columbia university, 1918. v, 118 p., 1 l.

Columbia university, 1917, PH. D.
Published also as Teachers college, Columbia university. Contributions to education, no. 89.
18–9794   BF431.R62

274 **Root, Francis Metcalf,** 1889–

Inheritance in the asexual reproduction of *Centropyxis aculeata* . . . [Princeton, N. J., 1918] cover-title, p. [173]–206.

Johns Hopkins university, 1917, PH. D.
"Reprinted from Genetics 3."
19–3994   QH431.R8

275 **Rost, Clayton Ord,** 1885–

Parallelism of the soils developed on the gray drifts of Minnesota . . . [Minneapolis?] 1918. 68 p.

University of Minnesota, 1918, PH. D.
19–27307   S593.R7

276 **Rowland, William Tingle,** 1881–

On the position in the clause of *ne* and *ut* in certain documents of colloquial Latin . . . New York, Columbia university press, 1918. 4 p. l., 44 p., 1 l.

(*Half-title:* Columbia university studies in classical philology)
Columbia university,   , PH. D.
Published also without thesis note.
20–530   PA2277.R7   1918a

277 **Sabin, Ethel Ernestine,** 1887–

William James and pragmatism . . . Lancaster, Pa., Press of the New era printing company [1918] v, 29, [1] p.

University of Illinois, 1916, PH. D.
Chapter I reprinted from the Journal of philosophy, psychology, and scientific methods. vol. XV, no. 12, June 6, 1918.
19–6026   B945.J24S3

278 **Sampson, Homer Cleveland.**
. . . Chemical changes accompanying abscission in
Coleus blumei . . . [Chicago, 1918]   1 p. l., p. 32–53.

University of Chicago, 1917, PH. D.

"Private edition, distributed by the University of Chicago libraries, Chicago, Illinois."

"Reprinted from the Botanical gazette, vol. LXVI, no. 1, July,
1918."

"Contributions from the Hull botanical laboratory 240."

18–22457   QK763.S3

279 **Schaffer, Aaron,** 1894–
Georg Rudolf Weckherlin, the embodiment of a transitional stage in German metrics. Chapter I. German metrics from earliest times to Opitz . . . Baltimore, J. H.
Furst company, 1918. 3 p. l., 57 p., 1 l.

Johns Hopkins university, 1917, PH. D.

"The complete monograph will be issued as number 10 of 'Hesperia: Studies in Germanic philology' edited by Profs. Hermann
Collitz and Henry Wood."

18–22819   PT1795.W3S3 1918

280 **Scholl, Clarence.**
The radioactivity of Illinois waters . . . [Urbana?
1918]   30 p., 1 l.

University of Illinois, 1916, PH. D.

18–18556   QC721.S4

281 **Scholz, Karl William Henry,** 1887–
. . . The art of translation, with special reference to
English renditions of the prose dramas of Gerhart
Hauptmann and Hermann Sudermann . . . Phila-
delphia, Pa., 1918.   5 p. l., 3–70 p.

(*Half-title:* Americana germanica. [no. 33])
University of Pennsylvania, 1918, PH. D.
Published also without thesis note.

18–8105   PT2616.Z9S5

282 **Schuette, Henry August.**
A biochemical study of the plankton of Lake Mendota
. . . [Madison, Wis.] 1918.   cover-title, p. 594–613.

University of Wisconsin, 1916, PH. D.

Thesis note stamped on cover.

"Reprinted from the Transactions of the Wisconsin academy of
sciences, arts, and letters, vol. XIX, part I."

19–27369   QL143.S3

283 **Schuetz, John Joseph,** 1874–
The origin of the teaching brotherhoods . . . Washington, **D.** C., 1918. 104 p.

Catholic university of America, 1918, PH. D.
19–2551   BX2813.S3

284 **Sell, Lewis Lazarus,** 1890–
De Catvlli carmine sexagesimo qvarto qvaestiones diversae . . . Novi Eboraci, ex officina W. D. Gray, 1918. 2 p. l., 110 p., 1 l.

Columbia university, 1918, PH. D.
19–1594   PA

285 **Shafer, Samuel Robert,** 1890–
The English ode to 1660; an essay in literary history . . . Princeton, Princeton university press; [etc., etc.] 1918. vi, 167 p.

Princeton university, 1916, PH. D.
18–20431   PR509.O3S5

286 **Shoemaker, Harry Melvin.**
. . . A generalized equation of the vibrating membrane expressed in curvilinear coordinates . . . Lancaster, Pa., Press of the New era printing company, 1918. iii, 18 p.

University of Pennsylvania, 1918, PH. D.
18–14650   QA935.S5

287 **Skinner, Glenn Seymour,** 1890–
XVIII. Molecular rearrangements in the camphor series. The decomposition products of the methyl ester of isoaminocamphonanic acid. A new reaction involving the formation of the methyl ether of a hydroxy acid . . . [Urbana? 1918] 31, [1] p.

University of Illinois, 1917, PH. D.
18–27180   QD416.S6

288 **Slaten, Arthur Wakefield.**
. . . Qualitative nouns in the Pauline Epistles and their translation in the revised version . . . Chicago, Ill., The University of Chicago press, 1918. 1 p. l., v–vii, 70 p.

University of Chicago, 1916, PH. D.
"Historical and linguistic studies, second series, vol. IV, part I."
18–22115   -   PA841.S52

289 **Sleator, William Warner,** 1883–
The absorption of near infra-red radiation by water-vapor . . . [Chicago, 1918] cover-title, p. 125–143.

University of Michigan, 1917, PH. D.
"Reprinted for private circulation from the Astrophysical journal, vol. XLVIII, no. 2, September 1918.".
19–2418 QC911.S6

290 **Smith, Frederick Madison,** 1874–
The higher powers of man . . . Lamoni, Ia., Printed by the Herald publishing house, 1918. 232 p.

Clark university, 1916, PH. D.
Published also without thesis note.
18–13262 BF408.S52

291 **Smith, Herbert Johnson.**
. . . On equilibrium in the system: ferrous carbonate, carbon dioxide and water. On equilibrium in the system: zinc carbonate, carbon dioxide and water. Equilibrium between alkali-earth carbonates, carbon dioxide and water . . . [Easton, Pa., 1918] 16 p.

University of Chicago, 1917, PH. D.
"Private edition, distributed by the University of Chicago libraries, Chicago, Illinois."
"Reprinted from the Journal of the American chemical society, vol. XL, no. 6, June, 1918."
19–7021 QD501.S65

292 **Snell, Ada Laura Fonda,** 1871–
. . . Pause; a study of its nature and its rhythmical function in verse, especially blank verse . . . Ann Arbor [The Ann Arbor press] 1918. 2 p. l., 85, [1] p.

(Contributions to rhetorical theory, ed. by F. N. Scott . . . VIII)
University of Michigan, 1916, PH. D.
18–13286 BF475.S6

293 **Snyder, Alice Dorothea,** 1887–
. . . The critical principle of the reconciliation of opposites as employed by Coleridge . . . Ann Arbor [The Ann Arbor press] 1918. 3 p. l., 59 p.

(Contributions to rhetorical theory, ed. by F. N. Scott . . . IX)
University of Michigan, 1915, PH. D.
Published also without thesis note.
19–2650 PR4484.S6

294 **Sperry, Pauline.**
. . . Properties of a certain projectively defined two-parameter family of curves on a general surface . . .
[Baltimore, 1918]   1 p. l., p. [213]–224.

University of Chicago, 1916, PH. D.
"Private edition distributed by the University of Chicago libraries, Chicago, Illinois, 1918."
"Reprinted from American journal of mathematics, vol. XL, no. 2, April, 1918."
18–11723   QA643.S7

295 **Stauffer, Vernon,** 1875–
New England and the Bavarian Illuminati . . . New York, 1918.   375 p.

Columbia university, 1918, PH. D.
Published also as Studies in history, economics and public law, ed. by the Faculty of political science of Columbia university, vol. LXXXII, no. 1, whole no. 191.
. 19–7334   F8.S79

296 **Stewart, Chester Arthur,** 1891–
Changes in the relative weights of the various parts, systems and organs of young albino rats underfed for various periods . . .   [Baltimore, 1918]   1 p. l., p. 301–353.

University of Minnesota, 1918, PH. D.
"Author's abstract of this paper issued by the [Wistar institute] Bibliographic service, February 2."
"Reprinted from the Journal of experimental zoölogy, volume 25, number 2, April, 1918."
18–23365   QP141.S69

297 **Stewart, John Quincy,** 1894–
The movement of momentum accompanying magnetic moment in iron and nickel . . .   Lancaster, Pa., Press of the New era printing co. [1918]   1 p. l., p. [100]–120.

Princeton university, 1919, PH. D.
"Reprinted from the Physical review, n. s., vol. XI, no. 2, February, 1918."
19–19255   QC631.S8

298 **Stock, Chester,** 1892–

The Pleistocene fauna of Hawver cave . . . [Berkeley, 1918] cover-title, p. [461]–515.

University of California, 1917, PH. D.
University of California publications. Bulletin of the Department of geology, v. 10, no. 24. Issued April 23, 1918, with a special thesis t.-p. dated May, 1917, attached to the cover-title.
18–13016   QE741.S7

299 **Stockett, Joseph Noble,** 1889–1916.

The arbitral determination of railway wages . . . Boston and New York, Houghton Mifflin company, 1918. xxv, 198, [2] p.

(*Half-title:* Hart, Schaffner & Marx prize essays. xxvi)
Johns Hopkins university, 1916, PH. D.
Published also without thesis note.
18–23376   HD5504.A3S7 1918a

300 **Stout, Joseph Duerson,** 1886–

On the motor functions of the cerebral cortex of the cat . . . Washington, D. C., 1918. cover-title, p. 177–229.

George Washington university, 1915, PH. D.
"Reprinted from Psychobiology, vol. I, no. 3, November, 1917."
20–1826   QP385.S7

301 **Stowell, Charles Jacob,** 1883–

The Journeymen tailors' union of America . . . [Urbana, 1918] 143, [1] p.

University of Illinois, 1917, PH. D.
"Reprinted from the University of Illinois studies in the social sciences, vol. VII, number 4, page 429, without changes in the text."
20–507   HD6515.T2S67

302 **Stuart, Henry Waldgrave,** 1871–

. . . Valuation as a logical process . . . [Chicago, 1918] 1 p. l., p. 227–340.

University of Chicago, 1900, PH. D.
"Private edition, distributed by the University of Chicago libraries, Chicago, Illinois."
"Reprinted from Studies in logical theory, by John Dewey."
18–17849   BD232.S8

303 **Sumner, Helen Laura,** 1876–
Citizenship (1827–1833) . . .

(*In* Commons, J. R. History of labour in the United States.   New York, 1918.   vol. I, pt. 2, p. [167]–332)
University of Wisconsin, 1908, PH. D.
Without thesis note.   HD8066.C7

304 **Swaine, James Malcolm,** 1878–
Canadian bark-beetles, a preliminary classification, with an account of the habits and means of control . . . [Ottawa, 1918]   2 p. l., 3–143 p.

Cornell university, 1919, PH. D.
"Reprinted from Canadian Department of agriculture, Entomological branch, Bulletin 14, part II, 1918."
19–7911   SB945.B3S8

305 **Swann, Harvey Julian,** 1884–
French terminologies in the making; studies in conscious contributions to the vocabulary . . .   New York, Columbia university press, 1918.   xxii, 250 p., 1 l.

(*Half-title:* Columbia university studies in Romance philology and literature)
Columbia university, 1918, PH D.
Published also without thesis note.
19–6717   PC2175.S82

306 **Tai, En-Sai,** 1894–
Treaty ports in China (a study in diplomacy) . . . New York city [University printing office, Columbia university] 1918.   x, 202 p., 1 l.   ·

Columbia university, 1918, PH. D.
Published also without thesis note.
18–6529   HF3776.T3   1918a

307 **Tanner, Fred Wilbur.**
A study of green fluorescent bacteria from water . . . [Baltimore, 1918]   2 p. l., 63–101 p., 1 l.

University of Illinois, 1916, PH. D.
"Reprinted from the Journal of bacteriology, vol. III, no. 1, January, 1918."
18–19307   QR84.T3

308 **Tarr, William Arthur.**
. . . The barite deposits of Missouri and the geology of
the barite district . . .   Columbia, Mo., University of
Missouri, 1918.   2 p. l., vii–xi, 111 p.

> University of Chicago, 1916, PH. D.
> "Science series, vol. III, no. 1, the University of Missouri studies."
> 18–22913   TN948.B18T3

309 **Taylor, John Prentice.**
The mythology of Vergil's Aeneid according to Servius . . .   [New York, 1918]   4 p. l., 62 p.

> New York university, 1917, PH. D.
> 18–13310   PA

310 **Taylor, Rood,** 1885–
Hunger in the infant . . .   [Minneapolis, 1918]   cover-title, 34 p.

> University of Minnesota, 1917, D. SC.
> 18–19494   QP141.T35

311 **Thrun, Walter Eugene,** 1892–
Determination of various forms of nitrogen in bovine
flesh, including the products of hydrolysis of some of the
proteins . . .   [Baltimore, 1918]   1 p. l., 22 p.

> University of Missouri, 1917, PH. D.
> "Reprinted from the Journal of biological chemistry, vol. XXXIV,
> no. 2, 1918."
> 19–27328   QP551.T5

312 **Thurston, Henry Winfred,** 1861–
Delinquency and spare time, a study of a few stories
written into the court records of the city of Cleveland
. . .   New York, 1918.   207 p.

> Columbia university, 1918, PH. D.
> Published also as Cleveland foundation.   Publication no. 27.
> 18–22989   HV9106.C6T6

313 **Tressler, Donald Kiteley,** 1894–
Solubility of soil potash in various salt solutions . . .
[Baltimore, 1918]   1 p. l., p. 237–257.

> Cornell university, 1918, PH. D.
> "Reprinted from Soil science, vol. 6, no. 3, September, 1918."
> 19–15846   S593.T7

314 **Tucker, Robert Leonard,** 1890–
The separation of the Methodists from the Church of England . . .   New York city, Printed by the Methodist book concern, 1918.   184 p., 1 l.

Columbia university, 1918, PH. D.
18–10165   BX8276.T8

315 **Ulrey, Clayton T.,** 1884–
. . . An experimental investigation of the energy in the continuous X-ray spectra of certain elements . . . Lancaster, Pa., Press of the New era printing company [1918]   1 p. l., p. [401]–410, 1 l.

(Phoenix physical laboratory contribution no. 40)
Columbia university, 1918, PH. D.
"Reprinted from the Physical review, vol. XI, no. 5, May, 1918."
18–23281   QC481.U5

316 **Ulrey, Dayton L.,** 1884–
The relation between the specific inductive capacity of an electrolyte and the electric potential of a metal placed in it . . .   Lancaster, Pa., Press of the New era printing company [1918]   1 p. l., p. [47]–58.

Leland Stanford junior university, 1917, PH. D.
"Reprinted from the Physical review, n. s., vol. XII, no. 1, July, 1918."
19–432   QD585.U3

317 **Vaeth, Joseph Anthony,** 1876–
Tirant lo Blanch; a study of its authorship, principal sources and historical setting . . .   New York, Columbia university press, 1918.   xvi, 169 p., 1 l.

(*Half-title:* Columbia university studies in Romance philology and literature)
Columbia university, 1917, PH. D.
Published also without thesis note.
19–6030   PC3937.T5V4

318 **Valleau, William Dorney,** 1891–
Sterility in the strawberry . . .   Washington, Govt. print. off., 1918.   cover-title, p. 613–670.

University of Minnesota, 1917, PH. D.
Thesis note mounted on p. 2 of cover.
"Reprinted from Journal of agricultural research, vol. XII, no. 10, Washington, D. C., March 11, 1918."
19–16521   QK827.V3

319 **Van den Broek, John A.,** 1885–

The effects of cold-working on the elastic properties of steel . . . [London, 1918] cover-title, 41 p.

University of Michigan, 1918, PH. D.
"Reprinted from the 'Journal of the Iron and steel institute,' London, England, of May, 1918."
19–2415   TA472.V3

Veazey, John Armor.

Kathodo-fluorescence of crystals, by Thomas B. Brown. Part I.—A quantitative investigation of the kathodo-fluorescence of willemite, kunzite, and soda glass. (A description of the results obtained by J. A. Veazey.) Part II.—A further investigation of willemite by the writer . . . Lancaster, Pa., Press of the New era printing company, 1918. 1 p. l., p. [39]–57.

"Part I is the substance of a thesis presented to the Faculty of the Graduate school of Cornell university by J. A. Veazey for the degree of doctor of philosophy."
"Part II is a thesis presented to the Faculty of the Graduate school of Cornell university by Thomas B. Brown for the degree of doctor of philosophy." 1916.
"Since the untimely death of J. A. Veazey prevented the immediate publication of his thesis, and since the work of the writer is so closely related to this previous work, these two papers are here issued as a single publication."
"Reprinted from Physical review, vol. XI, no. 1, January, 1918."
18–14649   QC477.B75

See 51 **Brown, Thomas Benjamin.**

320 **Visher, Stephen Sargent.**

. . . The geography of South Dakota . . . [Vermillion, S. D., 1918] 4 p. l., [7]–189 p.

University of Chicago, 1914, PH. D.
"Private edition, distributed by the University of Chicago libraries, Chicago, Illinois."
"Reprinted from South Dakota state Geological survey, Bulletin no. 8, July, 1918."
19–12002   F651.V82

321 **Vollmer, Clement.**

. . . The American novel in Germany, 1871–1913 . . . Philadelphia, International printing co., 1918. 3 p. l., [9]–94 p.

University of Pennsylvania, 1915, PH. D.
18–15774   PS159.G3V7

322 **Vollweiler, Ernest Henry**, 1893–

The action of acid halides on aldehydes and ketones
. . . [Easton, Pa., 1918]   19, [1] p.

University of Illinois, 1918, PH. D.
"Reprinted from the Journal of the American chemical society, vol.
XL, no. 11, p. 1732."

19–15859   QD341.A6V75

323 **Voss, Vivian**, 1894–

The ratio of the intensities of the D lines of sodium
. . . [Lancaster, Pa., Press of the New era printing
company, 1918]   1 p. l., p. [21]–28, 1 l.

Johns Hopkins university, 1917, PH. D.
"Reprinted from the Physical review, n. s., vol. XI, no. 1, January, 1918."

18–7748   QC462.S6V6

324 **Waksman, Selman Abraham**, 1888–

Studies on proteolytic activities of soil microorganisms . . . [Baltimore, 1918]   2 pt.

University of California, 1917, PH. D.
Reprints from the Journal of bacteriology, vol. III, no. 5, September, 1918; no. 6, November, 1918, issued as thesis, with thesis t.–p.
mounted on cover of pt. 1.
[Pt. 1] has title: Studies on proteolytic activities of soil microörganisms, with special reference to *Fungi*. [Pt. 2] Studies on the
proteolytic enzymes of soil *Fungi* and *Actinomycetes*.

19–8562   QR111.W2

325 **Waldron, Ralph Augustus.**

The peanut (*Arachis hypogea*); its history, histology,
physiology, and utility . . .   Philadelphia, Pa., 1918.
cover-title, p. [301]–338.

University of Pennsylvania, 1918, PH. D.
Reprinted from University of Pennsylvania Botanical contributions, vol. IV.

18–15696   SB351.P3W3

326 **Wang, Ching Chun**, 1883–

. . . Legislative regulation of railway finance in
England . . .   Urbana, 1918.   3 p. l., 9–196 p., 1 l.

University of Illinois, 1911, PH. D.
"Reprinted from the University of Illinois studies in the social
sciences, vol. VII, nos. 1 and 2."

19–27037   HE3017.W4

327 **Wann, Louis.**
The Oriental in Elizabethan drama . . . [Chicago,
1915] cover-title, p. 163–187.

University of Wisconsin, 1919, PH. D.
Part I of thesis.
"Reprinted for private circulation from Modern philology, vol. XII,
no. 7, January 1915."
Thesis note stamped on cover of pt. I.
20–3176 PR658.O7W3

Wann, Louis.
The Oriental in restoration drama . . . [Madison,
Wis., 1918] cover-title, p. [163]–186.

University of Wisconsin, 1919, PH. D.
Part II of thesis.
"Reprinted from University of Wisconsin studies in language and
literature number 2."
20–3175 PR658.O7W3

328 **Wardle, Addie Grace.**
. . . History of the Sunday school movement in the
Methodist Episcopal church . . . New York, Cincin-
nati, The Methodist book concern, 1918. 232 p.

University of Chicago, 1915, PH. D.
Published also without thesis note.
18–12997 BX8221.W32

329 **Warner, Earle Horace,** 1889–
The pressure increase in the corona . . . Lancaster,
Pa., Press of the New era printing company, 1918.
17, [1] p.

University of Illinois, 1918, PH. D.
"Reprinted from the Physical review, n. s., vol. VIII., no. 3,
September, 1916; and vol. X., no. 5, November, 1917."
18–19477 QC643.W3

330 **Watkins, Gordon,** 1889–
. . . A survey of the revenue system of Delaware
County, Pennsylvania, with especial reference to the
methods of assessment and collection of taxes . . .
Champaign, Ill., Flanigan-Pearson co., 1918. 2 p. l.,
80 p.

University of Pennsylvania, 1918, PH. D.
18–6530 HJ9307.D42W3

331 **Watson, Arthur Clinton.**
. . . The logic of religion . . . [Chicago, 1918]
iii, 99 p.

> University of Chicago, 1915, PH. D.
> "Private edition, distributed by the University of Chicago libraries, Chicago, Illinois."
> "Reprinted from the American journal of theology, vol. XX, nos. 1, 2, January, April, 1916; vol. XXII, nos. 2, 3, 4, April, July, October, 1918."
> 19–19948   BL51.W3

332 **Waynick, Dean David,** 1891–
The chemical composition of the plant as further proof of the close relation between antagonism and cell permeability . . .   [Berkeley, 1918]   cover-title, p. [135]–242.

> University of California, 1917, PH. D.
> University of California publications in agricultural sciences, v. 3, no. 8, July 12, 1918, with a special thesis t.-p. dated May 1917, attached to the cover-title.
> 18–19478   QK746.W3

333 **Wearing, Thomas.**
. . . The world-view of the fourth Gospel, a genetic study . . .   Chicago, Ill., The University of Chicago press, 1918.   2 p. l., 74 p.

> University of Chicago, 1917, PH. D.
> 18–19387   BS2615.W35

334 **Weatherwax, Paul.**
The evolution of maize . . . [New York, 1918] cover-title, p. 309–342.

> Indiana university, 1918, PH. D.
> Without thesis note.
> "Reprinted . . . from the Bulletin of the Torrey botanical club 45 . . . September 9, 1918."
> 20–9681   QK495.G74W4

335 **Weiland, Henry Joseph.**
The measurement of the conductivity of electrolytes in very dilute solutions . . .   [Urbana? 1918]   25, [1] p.

> University of Illinois, 1917, PH. D.
> 19–27038   QD565.W

336 **Weinstein, Alexander,** 1893–

Coincidence of crossing over in *Drosophila melanogaster* (*Ampelophila*) . . . [Princeton, N. J., 1918] cover-title, p. [135]–159.

Columbia university, 1917, PH. D.
"Reprinted from Genetics 3 . . . March, 1918."
18–15639   QH605.W4

337 **Weinstein, Israel.**

Extracts of antibodies obtained from specific precipitates of typhoid-antityphoid serum complex . . . [Baltimore, 1918] cover-title, p. 17–33.

New York university, 1917, D. SC.
"From the laboratory of bacteriology and hygiene, New York university, New York city."
"Reprinted from the Journal of immunology, vol. III, no. 1, January, 1918."
18–7767   QR185.W4

338 **Weiss, Charles.**

. . . The properties of pneumotoxin and its probable function in the pathology of lobar pneumonia . . . [Boston, 1918] 2 p. l., p. 103–122.

University of Pennsylvania, 1918, PH. D.
With a t.-p. and dedication [1919?] prefixed.
"Reprinted from the Journal of medical research, vol. XXXIX, no. 1 September, 1918."
20–3148   QR201.P7W4

339 **Wells, Bertram Whittier.**

. . . The zoocecidia of northeastern United States and eastern Canada . . . [Chicago, 1918] 1 p. l., p. 535–542.

University of Chicago, 1917, PH. D.
"Private edition, distributed by the University of Chicago libraries, Chicago, Illinois."
"Reprinted from the Botanical gazette, vol. LXV, no. 6, June, 1918."
"Contributions from the Hull botanical laboratory 239."
18–21624   SB767.W4

340 **Welo, Lars Alvin,** 1888–

On the variations of the photo-electric current due to heating and the occlusion and emission of gases . . . [Ithaca, N. Y., 1918] cover-title, p. [251]–276.

University of California, 1918, PH. D.
Reprint from the Physical review, n. s., vol. XII, no. 4, October, 1918, with a special thesis t.-p. dated May, 1918, attached to the cover-title.
18–23454   QC715.W4

341 **Wendel, Hugo Christian Martin.**
. . . The evolution of industrial freedom in Prussia, 1845–1849 . . . Allentown, Pa., H. R. Haas & co., 1918. 110 p.

> University of Pennsylvania, 1918, PH. D.
> 18–13017   HD3616.G45P85

342 **Weniger, Wanda.**
. . . Fertilization in *Lilium* . . . [Chicago, 1918] 1 p. l., p. 259–268.

> University of Chicago, 1918, PH. D.
> "Private edition, distributed by the University of Chicago libraries, Chicago, Illinois."
> "Reprinted from the Botanical gazette, vol. LXVI, no. 3, September, 1918."
> "Contributions from the Hull botanical laboratory 243."
> 18–22456   QK827.W4

343 **Whaling, Heiskell Bryan.**
. . . Fair value—economic and legal principles . . . Madison, Wis., 1918. 123 p.

> (Bulletin of the University of Wisconsin, no. 923. Economics and political science series, v. 9, no. 3)
> University of Wisconsin, 1915, PH. D.
> 19–27371   H31.W63   vol. 9, no. 3

344 **White, Earl Archibald,** 1883–
A study of the plow bottom and its action upon the furrow slice . . . [Washington, D. C., 1918] 1 p. l., 149–182 p., 1 l., [2] p., 1 l.

> Cornell university, 1917, PH. D.
> "Reprinted from Journal of agricultural research, vol. XII, no. 4, January 28, 1918."
> 19–6818   S683.W5

345 **White, Edith Grace,** 1890–
. . . The origin of the electric organs in *Astroscopus guttatus* . . . [Washington, D. C., 1918] p. [139]–172.

> Columbia university, 1918, PH. D.
> "Extracted from Publication no. 252 of the Carnegie institution of Washington, 1918."
> 18–7754   QP348.W5

346 **Whiteford, Gilbert Hayes,** 1876–
A study of the decomposition of silicates by barium
salts . . . Fort Collins, Colo., Courier press [1918]
26 p.

Johns Hopkins university, 1917, PH. D.
18–7523   QD181.S6W6

347 **Wiggans, Cleo Claude,** 1889–
. . . A study of some factors influencing fruitfulness
in apples . . . Columbia, University of Missouri, 1918.
60 p.

University of Missouri, 1918, PH. D.
Reprinted from the Missouri agricultural experiment station Research bulletin 32.
19–27327   SB363.W64

348 **Williams, Gertha,** 1884–
. . . The problem of restoration; a clinical study . . .
Menasha, Wis., George Banta publishing company, 1918.
2 p. l., 117 p.

University of Pennsylvania, 1917, PH. D.
18–3792   LC4019.W5

349 **Wilson, Benjamin Dunbar,** 1888–
The translocation of calcium in a soil . . . [Ithaca,
N. Y., 1918] 1 p. l., p. 295–324.

Cornell university, 1918, PH. D.
"Reprinted from Memoir 17, December, 1918, of Cornell university
agricultural experiment station."
19–8003   S593.W8

350 **Wilson, William Harold,** 1892–
On a certain general class of functional equations . . .
[Baltimore, 1918] 2 p. l., 20 p., 1 l.

University of Illinois, 1917, PH. D.
Reprinted from American journal of mathematics, v. 40, no. 3, July,
1918, p. 263–282.
19–4923   QA431.W6

351 **Woltman, Henry William,** 1889–
Brain changes associated with pernicious anemia . . .
Chicago, American medical association, 1918. cover-
title, 56 p.

University of Minnesota, 1917, PH. D.
"Reprinted from the Archives of internal medicine, June, 1918,
vol. XXI, pp. 791–838."
18–22187   RC641.W8

352 **Woods, William Colcord,** 1893–
The biology of alder flea-beetle . . . [Orono, Me., 1917] 1 p. l., p. [249]–284.

> Cornell university, 1917, PH. D.
> Pt. I of thesis.
> "Reprinted from Bulletin 265 of the Maine agricultural station."
> 19–15844   QL596.C5W63

Woods, William Colcord, 1893–
The alimentary canal of the larva of the alder flea-beetle . . . [Columbus, O., 1918] 1 p. l., p. 283–313.

> Cornell university, 1917, PH. D.
> Pt. II of thesis.
> "Reprinted from the Annals of the Entomological society of America, vol. XI, no. 3, September, 1918."
> 19–16515   QL596.C5W6

353 **Woodward, Alvalyn Eunice,** 1884–
Studies on the physiological significance of certain precipitates from the egg secretions of *Arbacia* and *Asterias* . . . [Baltimore, 1918] 1 p. l., p. 459–501.

> University of Michigan, 1918, PH. D.
> "Reprinted from the Journal of experimental zoölogy, volume 26, number 3, August, 1918."
> "Author's abstract of this paper issued by the [Wistar institute] Bibliographic service, June 24."
> 19–2419   QH485.W6

354 **Wooley, Elmer Otto.**
The sphere of music and musical terms in Goethe's lyric poems . . . Bloomington, Ind., 1918. 90 p.

> Indiana university, 1915, PH. D.
> 19–5288   PT2232.W7

355 **Wright, Winthrop Robins,** 1888–
The magnetization of iron in the absence of hysteresis . . . [Lancaster, Pa., and Ithaca, N. Y., 1918] cover-title, p. 161–169.

> University of Michigan, 1917, PH. D.
> "Reprinted from the Physical review, n. s., vol. XI, no. 3, March, 1918."
> 18–13015   QC761.W85

356 **Yerkes, Royden Keith.**
. . . The Lucianic version of the Old Testament as illustrated from Jeremiah 1–3 . . . [Middletown, Conn., 1918] 1 p. l., p. [163]–192.

University of Pennsylvania, 1918, PH. D.
"Reprinted from the Journal of Biblical literature XXXVII (1918), III–IV."
19–16639   BS64.L8Y4

357 **Yocom, Harry Barclay,** 1888–
The neuromotor apparatus of *Euplotes patella* . . . [Berkeley, 1918] cover-title, p. [337]–396.

University of California, 1917, PH. D.
University of California publications in zoology, v. 18, no. 14, September 7, 1918, with special thesis t.-p. dated December 1917 attached to the cover-title.
18–20527   QL368.C5Y7

358 **Young, Charles Otis.**
Tetrabromophthalic acid and some derivatives of tetrabromophthalimide . . . Pittsburgh, Pa., 1918. 16 p.

University of Pittsburgh,   , PH. D.
"Reprinted from the Journal of the American chemical society, September, 1918."
21–638   QD341.A2Y7

359 **Young, Vive Hall.**
Some factors affecting inulase formation in *Aspergillus niger* . . . [Baltimore, 1918] cover-title, p. 75–87, 114–133.

University of Wisconsin, 1916, PH. D.
Thesis note stamped on cover.
"Reprinted from the Plant world, vol. 21, nos. 4 and 5, April and May, 1918."
20–1825   QK896.Y6

360 **Zeydel, Edwin Hermann,** 1893–
The Holy Roman empire in German literature . . . New York, Columbia university press, 1918. ix, 144 p.

(*Half-title:* Columbia university Germanic studies)
Columbia university, 1918, PH. D.
Published also without thesis note.
19–10387   PT134.H7Z4 1918a

SECTION II

CLASSIFIED LISTS OF
THE THESES OF 1918, ARRANGED UNDER
THE BROAD CLASSES OF THE
LIBRARY OF CONGRESS
SCHEME

The 13 titles supplementary to the lists of 1914, 1916, and
1917 are included

91

CLASSIFIED LISTS OF THE THESES OF 1918, ARRANGED UNDER THE BROAD CLASSES OF THE LIBRARY OF CONGRESS SCHEME

The 13 titles supplementary to the lists of 1914, 1916, and 1917 are included.

Entries are given in same form as in Section I; titles are repeated if theses treat of more than one subject and the subjects belong to different classes.

A somewhat minute subject index can be found in Section III following.

Philosophy, Religion

(Class B)

Ayres, Clarence Edwin.
. . . The nature of the relationship between ethics and economics . . . Chicago, Ill., The University of Chicago press, 1918. 1 p. l., v–ix, 58 p.

University of Chicago, 1917, PH. D.
''Philosophic studies no. 8.''

Balz, Albert George Adam, 1887–
Idea and essence in the philosophies of Hobbes and Spinoza . . . New York, Columbia university press, 1918. 2 p. l., 86 p., 1 l.

Columbia university, 1916, PH. D.
Published also as Archives of philosophy, no. 10.

Beardslee, John Walter, 1879–
. . . The use of φύσις in fifth-century Greek literature . . . Chicago, Ill., The University of Chicago press, 1918. v, 126 p.

University of Chicago, 1913, PH. D.

Benda, Theodore.
Mental factors in the causation, cure and prevention of disease . . . [Worcester? Mass., 1918] 90 p.

Clark university, 1917, PH. D.

Blechman, Nathan.

The philosophic function of value; a study of experience showing the ultimate meaning of evolution to be the attainment of personality through culture and religion. Boston, R. G. Badger [°1918] 3 p. l., v–xv p., 1 l., 15–148 p.

(*Lettered on cover:* Studies in philosophy)
New York university, 1917, PH. D.
Thesis note on verso of t.-p.

Bock, Carl William, 1888–

The association of voluntary movements . . . [Baltimore, 1918] 1 p. l., p. 277–318, 1 l.

Ohio state university, 1917, PH. D.
"Reprinted from Psychobiology, vol. I, no. 4, January, 1918."

Bossard, James Herbert.

. . . The churches of Allentown; a study in statistics . . . Allentown, Pa., Jacks, the printer, 1918. 116 p.

University of Pennsylvania, 1918, PH. D.

Boström, Otto Henry, 1889–

. . . Alternative readings in the Hebrew of the books of Samuel . . . Pub. by the authority of the Board of directors of Augustana college and theological seminary, Rock Island, Illinois. Rock Island, Ill., Augustana book concern, printers, 1918. 60 p.

(Augustana library publications no. 8)
Yale university, 1916, PH. D.
Without thesis note.

Brandenburg, George Clinton.

Psychological aspects of language . . . [Baltimore, 1918] cover-title, p. 313–332.

University of Wisconsin, 1915, PH. D.
Thesis note stamped on cover.
"Reprint from the Journal of educational psychology, vol. IX, no. 6, June, 1918."

Bridgman, Olga Louise, 1886–

An experimental study of abnormal children, with special reference to the problems of dependency and delinquency . . . [Berkeley, 1918] cover-title, 59 p.

University of California, 1915, PH. D.
University of California publications in psychology, v. 3, no. 1, March 30, 1918, with a special thesis t.-p. dated May, 1915, attached to the cover-title.

Brockbank, Thomas William.
Redintegration in the albino rat, a study in retention . . . Washington, D. C., 1918. 2 p. l., 66 p.

Catholic university of America, 1918, PH. D.
Published also as Behavior monographs, v. 4, no. 2, serial no. 18.

Burchett, Bessie Rebecca.
. . . Janus in Roman life and cult, a study in Roman religions . . . Menasha, Wis., George Banta publishing company, 1918. 4 p. l., 75 p.

University of Pennsylvania, 1913, PH. D.

Campbell, Ivy Gertrude.
Manaism; a study in the psychology of religion . . . [Worcester, 1918] 1 p. l., 49 p.

Clark university, 1914, PH. D.
"Reprinted from the American journal of psychology, January, 1918, vol. XXIX."

Clark, Helen, 1890–
Visual imagery and attention: an analytical study . . . [Worcester, Mass., 1916] 2 p. l., p. [461]–492, 1 l.

University of Illinois, 1916, PH. D.
With a t.-p. and Contents [1918?] prefixed.
"Reprinted from the American journal of psychology, October, 1916, vol. XXVII."

Cornell, Clare Brown.
"A graduated scale for determining mental age" . . . [Frankfort, Ky., State journal co., 1918] 41 p.

University of Nebraska, 1915, PH. D.

Dodson, John Dillingham.
An experimental study of the relative values of reward and punishment in habit formation . . . [Baltimore, 1917] cover-title, p. 231–276.

University of Minnesota, 1918, PH. D.
"Reprinted from Psychobiology, vol. 1, no. 3, November, 1917."

Fortune, Alonzo Willard.
. . . The conception of authority in the Pauline writings . . . Chicago, Ill., 1918. 2 p. l., 183 p.

University of Chicago, 1915, PH. D.
"Private edition distributed by the University of Chicago libraries."

Fukuya, Shoan Masuzo.
. . . An experimental study of attention from the stand-point of mental efficiency: a contribution to educational and social problems . . . [Princeton, Princeton university press, 1918] 3 p. l., 42 p.

University of Chicago, 1917, PH. D.
"Private edition distributed by the University of Chicago libraries, Chicago, Illinois."
"Reprinted from the Psychological monographs, vol. xxv, whole no. 110, 1918."

Garth, Thomas Russell, 1872–
Mental fatigue during continuous exercise of a single function . . . [New York] 1918. ix, 85 p., 1 l.

Columbia university, 1918, PH. D.
Published also as Columbia university contributions to philosophy and psychology, vol. xxvi, no. 2 (Archives of psychology, no. 41)

Goudge, Mabel Ensworth, 1885–
A qualitative and quantitative study of Weber's illusion . . . [Worcester, Mass., 1918] 1 p. l., p. 81–119.

Cornell university, 1914, PH. D.
"Reprinted from the American journal of psychology, January, 1918, vol. xxix."

Hamilton, Arthur, 1886–
Sources of the religious element in Flaubert's Salammbô . . . Baltimore, The Johns Hopkins press, 1918. 1 p. l., 32 p., 1 l.

Johns Hopkins university, 1914, PH. D.
"An incomplete reprint from the Elliott monographs, no. 4."

Heider, Andrew Bernard, 1880–
The blessed Virgin Mary in early Christian Latin poetry . . . Washington, D. C., 1918. 79, [1] p.

Catholic university of America, 1918, PH. D.

Hewitt, Theodore Brown.
Paul Gerhardt as a hymn writer and his influence on English hymnody . . . New Haven, Yale university press; [etc., etc.] 1918. xiv p., 1 l., 169 p.

"Presented to the Faculty of the Graduate school of Yale university in candidacy for the degree of doctor of philosophy in June, 1917."—Pref.

Higby, Chester Penn, 1885–
The religious policy of the Bavarian government during the Napoleonic period . . . New York, 1918. 1 p. l., 5–347 p.

Columbia university, 1919, PH. D.
Published also as Studies in history, economics and public law, ed. by the Faculty of political science of Columbia university, vol. LXXXV, no. 1, whole no. 196.

Hoashi, Riichiro.
. . . The problem of omnipotence in current theology . . . Chicago, Ill., 1918. 2 p. l., 113 p.

University of Chicago, 1917, PH. D.
"Private edition, distributed by the University of Chicago libraries."

Hotz, Henry Gustave, 1880–
First year algebra scales . . . New York city, Teachers college, Columbia university, 1918. 3 p. l., 87, [1] p.

Columbia university, 1918. PH. D.

Ide, Gladys Genevra.
. . . The Witmer formboard and cylinders as tests for children two to six years of age . . . Philadelphia, Pa., The Psychological clinic press, 1918. 2 p. l., 24 p.

University of Pennsylvania, 1918, PH. D.
"Reprinted from the Psychological clinic, vol. XII, no. 3, May 15, 1918."

Kahn, Lina, 1887–
Metaphysics of the supernatural as illustrated by Descartes . . . New York, Columbia university press, 1918. viii, 65, [1] p., 1 l.

Columbia university, 1916, PH. D.
Published also as Archives of philosophy, no. 9.

Kelly, Caleb Guyer, 1887–
French Protestantism, 1559–1562 . . . Baltimore, 1918. viii, 9–186 p.

Johns Hopkins university, 1916, PH. D.
Published also as Johns Hopkins university studies in history and political science, series XXXVI, no. 4.

33564°—21——7

Kephart, Adam Perry, 1883–

. . . Clinical studies of failures with the Witmer formboard . . . Philadelphia, The Psychological clinic press,
1918. 1 p. l., p. 229–253.

University of Pennsylvania, 1918, PH. D.
"Reprinted from the Psychological clinic, vol. XI, no. 8, January, 1918."

Lamprecht, Sterling Power, 1890–

The moral and political philosophy of John Locke . . .
New York, Columbia university press, 1918. viii, 168 p., 1 l.

Columbia university, 1918, PH. D.
"Reprinted from Archives of philosophy, no. 11."

Levi, Gerson Benedict.

Gnomic literature in Bible and Apocrypha, with special
reference to the gnomic fragments and their bearing on
the proverb collections . . . [Philadelphia? 1918] 1 p. l.,
7–113 p.

University of Pennsylvania, 1910, PH. D.

McCann, Mary Agnes, *sister,* 1851–

Archbishop Purcell and the archdiocese of Cincinnati, a
study based on original sources . . . Washington, D. C.,
1918. 108 p.

Catholic university of America, 1918, PH. D.

Mateer, Florence.

Child behavior; a critical and experimental study of young
children by the method of conditioned reflexes . . . Boston,
R. G. Badger [1918] 2 p. l., 7–239 p.

Clark university, 1916, PH. D.
Published also without thesis note.

Mayer, Eli, 1880–

. . . War and religion; a sociological study . . . Philadelphia, Pa., 1918. 100 p.

University of Pennsylvania, 1918, PH. D.

Messer, William Stuart, 1882–

The dream in Homer and Greek tragedy . . . New York,
Columbia university press, 1918. viii p., 1 l., 105, [1] p.

(*Half-title:* Columbia university studies in classical philology)
Columbia university, 1918, PH. D.
Published also without thesis note.

Paschal, Franklin Cressey, 1890–
. . . The Witmer cylinder test . . . Hershey, Pa., The Hershey press, 1918. 54 p.

University of Pennsylvania, 1918, PH. D.

Peters, Charles Clinton, 1887–
. . . Selection and organization of materials for a course in "the control of conduct" for secondary schools . . . Spring City, Pa., The Interborough press [1918] 120 p.

University of Pennsylvania, 1916, PH. D.

Ridgley, Frank Harris.
Jewish ethical idealism . . . Boston, The Gorham press, 1918. 97 p.

University of Pennsylvania, 1916, PH. D.
Published also without thesis note in the Library of religious thought.

Roesch, *Sister* **Mary Jeanette,** 1884–
Vocational preparation of youth in Catholic schools . . . Washington, D. C., 1918. 73 p.

Catholic university of America, 1918, PH. D.

Rogers, Agnes Low, 1884–
Experimental tests of mathematical ability and their prognostic value . . . New York city, Teachers college, Columbia university, 1918. v, 118 p., 1 l.

Columbia university, 1917, PH. D.
Published also as Teachers college, Columbia university. Contributions to education, no. 89.

Sabin, Ethel Ernestine, 1887–
William James and pragmatism . . . Lancaster, Pa., Press of the New era printing company [1918] v, 29, [1] p.

University of Illinois, 1916, PH. D.
Chapter I reprinted from the Journal of philosophy, psychology, and scientific methods. vol. XV, no. 12, June 6, 1918.

Schuetz, John Joseph, 1874–
The origin of the teaching brotherhoods . . . Washington, D. C., 1918. 104 p.

Catholic university of America, 1918, PH. D.

Slaten, Arthur Wakefield.

. . . Qualitative nouns in the Pauline Epistles and their translation in the revised version . . . Chicago, Ill., The University of Chicago press, 1918. 1 p. l., v–vii, 70 p.

University of Chicago, 1916, PH. D.
"Historical and linguistic studies, second series, vol. IV, part I."

Smith, Frederick Madison, 1874–

The higher powers of man . . . Lamoni, Ia., Printed by the Herald publishing house, 1918. 232 p.

Clark university, 1916, PH. D.
Published also without thesis note.

Snell, Ada Laura Fonda, 1871–

. . . Pause; a study of its nature and its rhythmical function in verse, especially blank verse . . . Ann Arbor [The Ann Arbor press] 1918. 2 p. l., 85, [1] p.

(Contributions to rhetorical theory, ed. by F. N. Scott . . . VIII)
University of Michigan, 1916, PH. D.

Stauffer, Vernon, 1875–

New England and the Bavarian Illuminati . . . New York, 1918. 375 p.

Columbia university, 1918, PH. D.
Published also as Studies in history, economics and public law, ed. by the Faculty of political science of Columbia university, vol. LXXXII, no. 1, whole no. 191.

Stuart, Henry Waldgrave, 1871–

. . . Valuation as a logical process . . . [Chicago, 1918] 1 p. l., p. 227–340.

University of Chicago, 1900, PH. D.
"Private edition, distributed by the University of Chicago libraries, Chicago, Illinois."
"Reprinted from Studies in logical theory, by John Dewey."

Taylor, John Prentice.

The mythology of Vergil's Aeneid according to Servius . . . [New York, 1918] 4 p. l., 62 p.

New York university, 1917, PH. D.

Tucker, Robert Leonard, 1890–

The separation of the Methodists from the Church of England . . . New York city, Printed by the Methodist book concern, 1918. 184 p., 1 l.

Columbia university, 1918, PH. D.

Wardle, Addie Grace.
. . . History of the Sunday school movement in the Methodist Episcopal church . . . New York, Cincinnati, The Methodist book concern, 1918. 232 p.

University of Chicago, 1915, PH. D.
Published also without thesis note.

Watson, Arthur Clinton.
. . . The logic of religion . . . [Chicago, 1918] iii, 99 p.

University of Chicago, 1915, PH. D.
"Private edition, distributed by the University of Chicago libraries, Chicago, Illinois."
"Reprinted from the American journal of theology, vol. XX, nos. 1, 2, January, April, 1916; vol. XXII, nos. 2, 3, 4, April, July, October, 1918."

Wearing, Thomas.
. . . The world-view of the fourth Gospel, a genetic study . . . Chicago, Ill., The University of Chicago press, 1918. 2 p. l., 74 p.

University of Chicago, 1917, PH. D.

Yerkes, Royden Keith.
. . . The Lucianic version of the Old Testament as illustrated from Jeremiah 1–3 . . . [Middletown, Conn., 1918] 1 p. l., p. [163]–192.

University of Pennsylvania, 1918, PH. D.
"Reprinted from the Journal of Biblical literature XXXVII (1918), III–IV."

History
(except American)

(Class D)

Boyce, Myrna M.
The diplomatic relations of England with the Quadruple alliance 1815–1830 . . . [Iowa City? 1918] 76 p.

University of Iowa, 1917, PH. D.
Published also as University of Iowa monographs, 1st ser., no. 22. November 1918.

Bradley, Harriett, 1892–
The enclosures in England, an economic reconstruction . . . New York, 1918. 3 p. l., 9–113 p.

Columbia university, 1917, PH. D.
Published also as Studies in history, economics, and public law, ed. by the Faculty of political science of Columbia university, vol. LXXX, no. 2, whole no. 186.

Fundenburg, George Baer, 1893–

Feudal France in the French epic, a study of feudal French institutions in history and poetry . . . Princeton, N. J., 1918. 4 p. l., 121 p.

Columbia university, 1919, PH. D.

Greenfield, Kent Roberts, 1893–

Sumptuary law in Nürnberg; a study in paternal government . . . Baltimore, 1918. v, 7–140 p.

Johns Hopkins university, 1915, PH. D.

Published also as Johns Hopkins university studies in historical and political science. ser. XXXVI, no. 2.

Higby, Chester Penn, 1885–

The religious policy of the Bavarian government during the Napoleonic period . . . New York, 1918. 1 p. l., 5–347 p.

Columbia university, 1919, PH. D.

Published also as Studies in history, economics and public law, ed. by the Faculty of political science of Columbia university, vol. LXXXV, no. 1, whole no. 196.

Jones, Paul Van Brunt.

. . . The household of a Tudor nobleman . . . Cedar Rapids, Ia., The Torch press, 1918. 5 p. l., 9–277 p.

University of Pennsylvania, 1912, PH. D.

"Reprinted from the University of Illinois studies in social sciences, volume VI, number 4."

Koller, Armin Hajman.

. . . The theory of environment, an outline of the history of the idea of milieu, and its present status. pt. I . . . Menasha, Wis., George Banta publishing company, 1918. 6 p. l., 104 p.

University of Chicago, 1911, PH. D.

Published also without thesis note.

Kraeling, Emil Gottlieb Heinrich, 1892–

. . . Aram and Israel; or, The Aramaeans in Syria and Mesopotamia . . . New York, Columbia university press, 1918. xvi, 155 p., 1 l.

(Columbia university oriental studies, vol. XIII)

Columbia university, 1917, PH. D.

Published also without thesis note.

Le Duc, Alma de Lande, 1878–

Gontier Col and the French pre-renaissance . . . New York, 1918. vii, 103, [1] p.

Columbia university, 1916, PH. D.
"Reprinted from the Romanic review, vol. VII, no. 4, 414–457, 1916; vol. VIII, no. 2, 145–165, and no. 3, 290–306, 1917."

Leffingwell, Georgia Williams, 1893–

Social and private life at Rome in the time of Plautus and Terence . . . New York, 1918. 2 p. l., 7–141 p.

Columbia university, 1918, PH. D.
Published also as Studies in history, economics, and public law, edited by the Faculty of political science of Columbia university. vol. LXXXI, no. 1; whole no. 188.

Mayer, Eli, 1880–

. . . War and religion; a sociological study . . . Philadelphia, Pa., 1918. 100 p.

University of Pennsylvania, 1918, PH. D.

Zeydel, Edwin Hermann, 1893–

The Holy Roman empire in German literature . . . New York, Columbia university press, 1918. ix, 144 p.

(*Half-title:* Columbia university Germanic studies)
Columbia university, 1918, PH. D.
Published also without thesis note.

America

(Classes E–F)

Coulter, Ellis Merton, 1890–

Effects of secession upon the commerce of the Mississippi Valley . . . [Cedar Rapids, 1916] cover-title, 1 p. l., p. [275]–300.

University of Wisconsin, 1917, PH. D.
Thesis note stamped on cover.
"Reprinted from the Mississippi Valley historical review, vol. III, no. 3, Dec. 1916."

Davidson, Gordon Charles, 1884–

The North West company . . . [Berkeley, 1918] cover-title, xi, 349 p.

University of California, 1916, PH. D.
University of California publications in history, vol. VII, with a special thesis t.-p., dated 1916, attached to the cover-title.

Ellinger, Esther Parker.

The southern war poetry of the civil war . . . Philadelphia, Pa. [Hershey, Pa., The Hershey press] 1918.   192 p.

. University of Pennsylvania, 1918, PH. D.

Fox, Dixon Ryan, 1887–

The decline of aristocracy in the politics of New York . . . New York, 1918.   xiii, 460 p., 1 l.

Columbia university, 1917, PH. D.

Published also as Studies in history, economics and public law, ed. by the Faculty of political science of Columbia university, vol. LXXXVI, whole no. 198.

Garrett, Mitchell Bennett, 1881–

The French colonial question 1789–1791; dealings of the Constituent assembly with problems arising from the revolution in the West Indies . . . Ann Arbor, Mich., G. Wahr [1918]   iv, p., 1 l., 167 p.

Cornell university, 1910, PH. D.

Published in 1916 without thesis note.

Hamer, Philip May.

. . . The secession movement in South Carolina, 1847–1852 . . . Allentown, Pa., H. R. Haas & co., 1918. v, 152 p.

University of Pennsylvania, 1918, PH. D.

Hollingsworth, William Wiley.

. . . Woodrow Wilson's political ideals as interpreted from his works . . . Princeton, Princeton university press, 1918.   vi, 53 p.

University of Pennsylvania, 1918, PH. D.

Johnson, Franklin, 1875–

The development of state legislation concerning the free negro . . . New York, 1918.   vi, 207, [1] p.

Columbia university, 1918, PH. D.

Published in 1919 without thesis note.

Lefferts, Walter, 1875–

. . . Tidewater Maryland, an embayed coast plain . . . Philadelphia, International printing company, 1918. 64 p.

University of Pennsylvania, 1918, PH. D.

Lonn, Ella.
. . . Reconstruction in Louisiana after 1868 . . . New York and London, G. P. Putnam's sons, 1918. 1 p. l., 95 p.

University of Pennsylvania, 1911, PH. D.
Comprises the first four chapters of a much larger work which was published without thesis note but with the same title.

Lowrey, Lawrence Tyndale, 1888–
Northern opinion of approaching secession, October, 1859–November, 1860 . . . Northampton, Mass., 1918. 2 p. l., p. [191]–258.

Columbia university, 1917, PH. D.

McDougle, Ivan Eugene.
Slavery in Kentucky, 1792–1865 . . . [Lancaster, Pa., Press of the New era printing company, 1918] 2 p. l., 125 p.

Clark university, 1918, PH. D.
"Reprinted from the Journal of negro history, vol. III, no. 3, July, 1918."

Martin, Asa Earl, 1885–
The anti-slavery movement in Kentucky prior to 1850 . . . Louisville? Ky., 1918] 165 p.

Cornell university, 1915, PH. D.
Published also as Filson club publication no. 29.

Munro, Dana Gardner.
. . . The five republics of Central America; their political and economic development and their relations with the United States . . . New York [etc.] Oxford university press, 1918. viii p., 1 l., 332 p.

University of Pennsylvania, 1917, PH. D.
Published also by the Carnegie endowment for international peace, Division of economics and history.

Musser, John.
. . . The establishment of Maximilian's empire in Mexico . . . Menasha, Wis., George Banta publishing company, 1918. 2 p. l., 100 p.

University of Pennsylvania, 1912, PH. D.

Noble, Stuart Grayson, 1886–
Forty years of the public schools in Mississippi, with special reference to the education of the negro . . . New York city,

Teachers college, Columbia university, 1918. iv p., 1 l.,
142 p., 1 l.

Columbia university, 1918, PH. D.

Published also as Contributions to education, Teachers college, Columbia
university, no. 94.

Parkins, Almon Ernest.

. . . The historical geography of Detroit . . . Chicago,
Ill., 1918. xix, 356 p.

University of Chicago, 1914, PH. D.

"A private edition distributed by the University of Chicago libraries."

"University series, III. The Michigan historical commission, Lansing,
Michigan."

Purcell, Richard Joseph.

Connecticut in transition, 1775–1818 . . . Washington,
American historical association; [etc., etc.] 1918. x, 471 p.

Yale university, 1916, PH. D.

Without thesis note.

"To this essay was awarded the Justin Winsor prize in American history
for 1916."

Putnam, James William.

. . . The Illinois and Michigan canal; a study in economic
history . . . Illinois centennial publication. Chicago, The
University of Chicago press, 1918. xiii, 213 p.

(Chicago historical society's collection, vol. x)

University of Wisconsin, 1909, PH. D.

Thesis note stamped on t.-p.

Reuter, Edward Byron.

. . . The mulatto in the United States, including a study
of the rôle of mixed-blood races throughout the world . . .
Boston, R. G. Badger, 1918. 1 p. l., 5–417 p.

University of Chicago, 1919, PH. D.

Published also without thesis note.

Stauffer, Vernon, 1875–

New England and the Bavarian Illuminati . . . New
York, 1918. 375 p.

Columbia university, 1918, PH. D.

Published also as Studies in history, economics and public law, ed. by
the Faculty of political science of Columbia university, vol. LXXXII, no. 1,
whole no. 191.

Visher, Stephen Sargent.
. . . The geography of South Dakota . . . [Vermillion, S. D., 1918] 4 p. l., [7]–189 p.

University of Chicago, 1914, PH. D.
"Private edition, distributed by the University of Chicago libraries, Chicago, Illinois."
"Reprinted from South Dakota state Geological survey, Bulletin no. 8, July, 1918."

Geography, Anthropology

(Class G)

Campbell, Ivy Gertrude.
Manaism; a study in the psychology of religion . . . [Worcester, 1918] 1 p. l., 49 p.

Clark university, 1914, PH. D.
"Reprinted from the American journal of psychology, January, 1918, vol. XXIX."

Koller, Armin Hajman.
. . . The theory of environment, an outline of the history of the idea of milieu, and its present status. pt. I
. . . Menasha, Wis., George Banta publishing company, 1918. 6 p. l., 104 p.

University of Chicago, 1911, PH. D.
Published also without thesis note.

Parkins, Almon Ernest.
. . . The historical geography of Detroit . . . Chicago, Ill., 1918. xix, 356 p.

University of Chicago, 1914, PH. D.
"A private edition distributed by the University of Chicago libraries."
"University series, III. The Michigan historical commission, Lansing, Michigan."

Reuter, Edward Byron.
. . . The mulatto in the United States, including a study of the rôle of mixed-blood races throughout the world . . . Boston, R. G. Badger, 1918. 1 p. l., 5–417 p.

University of Chicago, 1919, PH. D.
Published also without thesis note.

Visher, Stephen Sargent.
. . . The geography of South Dakota . . . [Vermillion, S. D., 1918]   4 p. l., [7]–189 p.

University of Chicago, 1914, PH. D.
"Private edition, distributed by the University of Chicago libraries, Chicago, Illinois."
"Reprinted from South Dakota state Geological survey, Bulletin no. 8, July, 1918."

Social Sciences

(Class H)

Andrews, John Bertram, 1880–
Nationalisation (1860–1877) . . .

(*In* Commons, J. R. History of labour in the United States. New York, 1918. vol. II, pt. 5, p. 1–191)
University of Wisconsin, 1908, PH. D.
Without thesis note.

Ayers, Clarence Edwin.
. . . The nature of the relationship between ethics and economics . . . Chicago, Ill., The University of Chicago press, 1918.   1 p. l., v–ix, 58 p.

University of Chicago, 1917, PH. D.
"Philosophic studies no. 8."

Barnes, Harry Elmer, 1889–
A history of the penal, reformatory and correctional institutions of the state of New Jersey, analytical and documentary . . . Trenton, N. J., MacCrellish & Quigley company, 1918.   654 p., 1 l.

Columbia university, 1918, PH. D.

Barron, Mary Louise, 1892–
. . . State regulation of the securities of railroads and public service companies . . . Philadelphia, 1918.   28 p.

University of Pennsylvania, 1917, PH. D.
"Reprinted from vol. LXXVI of the Annals of the American academy of political and social science."

Bradley, Harriett, 1892–
The enclosures in England, an economic reconstruction
. . . New York, 1918.   3 p. l., 9–113 p.

Columbia university, 1917, PH. D.
Published also as Studies in history, economics and public law, ed. by
the Faculty of political science of Columbia university, vol. LXXX, no. 2,
whole no. 186.

Cotterill, Robert Spencer, 1884–
Southern railroads and western trade, 1840–1850.

(*In* Mississippi Valley historical review.   Cedar Rapids, Ia., 1917.   vol.
III, no. 4, p. [427]–441)
University of Wisconsin, 1919, PH. D.
Part I of thesis.
Without thesis note.

Cotterill, Robert Spencer, 1884–
Memphis railroad convention, 1849.

(*In* Tennessee historical magazine.   Nashville, 1918.   vol. 4, no. 2,
p. [83]–94)
University of Wisconsin, 1919, PH. D.
Part II of thesis.
Without thesis note.

Cotterill, Robert Spencer, 1884–
The national railroad convention in St. Louis, 1849 . . .
(*In* Missouri historical review.   Columbia, 1918.   vol. XII, no. 4, p. 203–
215)
University of Wisconsin, 1919, PH. D.
Part III of thesis.
Without thesis note.

Coulter, Ellis Merton, 1890–
Effects of secession upon the commerce of the Mississippi
Valley . . . [Cedar Rapids, 1916]   cover-title, 1 p. l., p.
[275]–300.

University of Wisconsin, 1917, PH. D.
Thesis note stamped on cover.
"Reprinted from the Mississippi Valley historical review, vol. III, no. 3,
Dec. 1916."

Davidson, Gordon Charles, 1884–
The North West company . . .   [Berkeley, 1918]   cover-
title, xi, 349 p.

University of California, 1916, PH. D.
University of California publications in history, vol. VII, with a special
thesis t.-p., dated 1916, attached to the cover-title.

Estcourt, Rowland Metzner, 1855–

. The conflict of tax laws . . . [Berkeley, 1918] cover-title, p. [115]–231.

University of California, 1916, PH. D.
University of California, publications in economics, v. 4, no. 3, April 2, 1918, with a special thesis t.-p. attached to the cover-title.

Ferguson, Maxwell, 1888–

State regulation of railroads in the South . . . New York, 1916. 2 p. l., 7–230 p.

Columbia university,   , PH. D.
Published also as Studies in history, economics and public law, ed. by the Faculty of political science of Columbia university. v. 67, no. 2; whole no. 162.

Florence, Philip Sargant, 1890–

Use of factory statistics in the investigation of industrial fatigue, a manual for field research . . . New York, 1918. 156 p.

Columbia university, 1918, PH. D.
, Published also as Studies in history, economics and public law, ed. by the Faculty of political science of Columbia university. vol. LXXXI, no. 3; whole no. 190.

Gallaher, Ruth Augusta, 1882–

Legal and political status of women in Iowa, an historical account of the rights of women in Iowa from 1838 to 1918 . . . Iowa City, Ia., 1918. xii, 300 p.

University of Iowa, 1918, PH. D.

Gowin, Enoch Burton, 1883–

The selection and training of the business executive . . . New York, The Macmillan company, 1918. xii p., 1 l., 225 p.

Columbia university, 1918, PH. D.

Greenfield, Kent Roberts, 1893–

Sumptuary law in Nürnberg; a study in paternal government . . . Baltimore, 1918. v, 7–140 p.

Johns Hopkins university, 1915, PH. D.
Published also as Johns Hopkins university studies in historical and political science. ser. XXXVI, no. 2.

Hale, Robert Lee, 1884–

Valuation and rate-making; the conflicting theories of the Wisconsin railroad commission, 1905–1917, with a chapter on the uncertainty of the United States Supreme court decisions, and a concluding chapter on the need of a revised principle of utility valuation . . . New York, 1918. 1 p. l., 5–157 p.

Columbia university, 1918, PH. D.

Published also as Studies in history, economics and public law, ed. by the Faculty of political science of Columbia university, vol. LXXX, no. 1, whole no. 185.

Haring, Clarence Henry.

Trade and navigation between Spain and the Indies in the time of the Hapsburgs . . . Cambridge, Harvard university press; [etc., etc.] 1918. xxviii, 371, [1] p.

(*Half-title:* Harvard economic studies . . . vol. XIX)

Harvard university, 1916, PH. D.

Without thesis note.

"Part of the material in chapter VII was embodied in an article printed in the Quarterly journal of economics, in May 1915, and the second half of chapter. VIII is largely an adaptation of another article, 'España y el Canal de Panamá,' which appeared in Hispania (London) in December 1912."—Pref.

Hayward, Percy Roy.

. . . Compensation for injuries to Canadian workmen . . . Toronto, Canada, Canada law book co., 1918. 1 p. l., p. [281]–335.

University of Pennsylvania, 1918, PH. D.

Reprinted from Canada law journal, v. 54, nos. 8–9, August–September, 1918.

Huang, Han Liang, 1893–

The land tax in China . . . New York, 1918. 2 p. l., 7–181 p.

Columbia university, 1918, PH. D.

Published also as Studies in history, economics and public law, ed. by the Faculty of political science of Columbia university. vol. LXXX, no. 3; whole no. 187.

Keddy, John Lewis, 1891–

The New York state legislative budget for 1917 . . . [New York, 1917] 2 p. l., iii–x, 141 p.

Columbia university, 1919, PH. D.

Published also as Municipal research, issued by the Bureau of municipal research, no. 86, June, 1917.

Kester, Roy Bernard, 1882–

A study in valuation of the commercial balance sheet (comprising Chapters IV to XXVII inclusive of this volume) [Accounting theory and practice vol. II] . . . New York, The Ronald press company, 1918. xxiv, 796 p.

Columbia university, 1919, PH. D.

Koller, Armin Hajman.

. . . The theory of environment, an outline of the history of the idea of milieu, and its present status. pt. I . . . Menasha, Wis., George Banta publishing company, 1918. 6 p. l., 104 p.

University of Chicago, 1911, PH. D.
Published also without thesis note.

Lefferts, Walter, 1875–

. . . Tidewater Maryland, an embayed coast plain . . . Philadelphia, International printing company, 1918. 64 p.

University of Pennsylvania, 1918, PH. D.

Lowe, Boutelle Ellsworth, 1890–

International aspects of the labor problem . . . N[ew] Y[ork] W. D. Gray [1918] 2 p. l., 3–128 p., 1 l.

Columbia university, 1918, PH. D.

Lutz, Harley Leist, 1882–

The state tax commission; a study of the development and results of state control over the assessment of property for taxation . . . Awarded the David A. Wells prize for the year 1915–16, and pub. from the income of the David A. Wells fund. Cambridge, Harvard university press; [etc., etc.] 1918. ix, 673, [1] p.

(*Half-title:* Harvard economic studies . . . vol. XVII)
"Submitted as a doctoral dissertation at Harvard in 1914, and is now published, after a thorough revision."—Pref.

Marvin, Donald Mitchell.

. . . Occupational propinquity as a factor in marriage selection . . . [Philadelphia?] 1918. 22 p.

University of Pennsylvania, 1918, PH. D.

Mayer, Eli, 1880–

. . . War and religion; a sociological study . . . Philadelphia, Pa., 1918. 100 p.

University of Pennsylvania, 1918, PH. D.

Morimoto, Kokichi, 1879–

The standard of living in Japan . . . Baltimore, 1918. vii, 9–147 p., 1 l.

Johns Hopkins university, 1916, PH. D.
Published also as Johns Hopkins university studies in historical and political science . . . ser. XXXVI, no. 1.

Munro, Dana Gardner.

. . . The five republics of Central America; their political and economic development and their relations with the United States . . . New York [etc.] Oxford university press, 1918. viii p., 1 l., 332 p.

University of Pennsylvania, 1917, PH. D.
Published also by the Carnegie endowment for international peace, Division of economics and history.

Noel, Francis Regis, 1891–

A history of the bankruptcy clause of the Constitution of the United States of America . . . [Gettysburg, Gettysburg compiler print, 1918] 210 p.

Catholic university of America, 1918, PH. D.

Northcott, Clarence Hunter, 1880–

Australian social development . . . New York, 1918. 2 p. l., 7–303 p., 1 l.

Columbia university, 1918, PH. D.
Published also as Studies in history, economics and public law, ed. by the Faculty of political science of Columbia university, vol. LXXXI, no. 2; whole no. 189.

Nourse, Edwin Griswold, 1883–

. . . The Chicago produce market; a study of market mechanism as a factor in price determination . . . Boston, Houghton Mifflin company, 1918. 6 p. l., 304 p., 1 l.

(*Half-title:* Hart, Schaffner & Marx prize essays. XXV)
University of Chicago, 1915, PH. D.
Published also without thesis note.

Paterson, Robert Gildersleeve.

. . . Wage payment legislation in the United States . . . [Washington, D. C.] 1918. 186 p.

University of Pennsylvania, 1909, PH. D.
Published also as Bulletin of the U. S. Bureau of labor statistics, whole no. 229.

Perlman, Selig.
Upheaval and reorganisation (since 1876) . . .

(*In* Commons, J. R. History of labour in the United States. New York, 1918. vol. II, pt. 6, p. [193]–537)
University of Wisconsin, 1915, PH. D.
Without thesis note.

Pollock, Ivan Lester, 1887–
History of economic legislation in Iowa . . . Iowa City, Ia., 1918. vi p., 1 l., 386 p.

University of Iowa, 1917, PH. D.
Published also in Iowa economic history series.

Powell, Fred Wilbur, 1881–
The recent movement for state budget reform: 1911–1917 . . . [New York, 1918] 2 p. l., iii–ix, 157 p.

Columbia university, 1918, PH. D.
"Reprinted from Municipal research, New York, November, 1917, no. 91."

Putnam, James William.
. . . The Illinois and Michigan canal; a study in economic history . . . Illinois centennial publication. Chicago, The University of Chicago press, 1918. xiii, 213 p.

(Chicago historical society's collection, vol. x)
University of.Wisconsin, 1909, PH. D.
Thesis note stamped on t.-p.

Quigley, Harold Scott.
. . . The immunity of private property from capture at sea . . . Madison, Wis., 1918. 200 p.

(Bulletin of the University of Wisconsin, no. 918. Economics and political science series, v. 9, no. 2)
University of Wisconsin, 1916, PH. D.

Stauffer, Vernon, 1875–
New England and the Bavarian Illuminati . . . New York, 1918. 375 p.

Columbia university, 1918, PH. D.
Published also as Studies in history, economics and public law, ed. by the Faculty of political science of Columbia university, vol. LXXXII, no. 1, whole no. 191.

Stockett, Joseph Noble, 1889–1916.

The arbitral determination of railway wages . . . Boston and New York, Houghton Mifflin company, 1918. xxv, 198, [2] p.

(*Half-title:* Hart, Schaffner & Marx prize essays. xxvi)
Johns Hopkins university, 1916, PH. D.
Published also without thesis note.

Stowell, Charles Jacob, 1883–

The Journeymen tailors' union of America . . . [Urbana, 1918] 143, [1] p.

University of Illinois, 1917, PH. D.
"Reprinted from the University of Illinois studies in the social sciences, vol. VII, number 4, page 429, without changes in the text."

Stuart, Henry Waldgrave, 1871–

. . . Valuation as a logical process . . . [Chicago, 1918] 1 p. l., p. 227–340.

University of Chicago, 1900, PH. D.
"Private edition, distributed by the University of Chicago libraries, Chicago, Illinois."
"Reprinted from Studies in logical theory, by John Dewey."

Sumner, Helen Laura, 1876–

Citizenship (1827–1833) . . .

(*In* Commons, J. R. History of labour in the United States. New York, 1918. vol I, pt. 2, p. [167]–332)
University of Wisconsin, 1908, PH. D.
Without thesis note.

Tai, En-Sai, 1894–

Treaty ports in China (a study in diplomacy) . . . New York city [University printing office, Columbia university] 1918. x, 202 p., 1 l.

Columbia university, 1918, PH. D.
Published also without thesis note.

Thurston, Henry Winfred, 1861–

Delinquency and spare time, a study of a few stories written into the court records of the city of Cleveland . . . New York, 1918. 207 p.

Columbia university, 1918, PH. D.
Published also as Cleveland foundation. Publications no. 27.

Wang, Ching Chun, 1883–

. . . Legislative regulation of railway finance in England . . . Urbana, 1918. 3 p. l., 9–196 p., 1 l.

University of Illinois, 1911, PH. D.
"Reprinted from the University of Illinois studies in the social sciences, vol. VII, nos. 1 and 2."

Watkins, Gordon, 1889–

. . . A survey of the revenue system of Delaware County, Pennsylvania, with especial reference to the methods of assessment and collection of taxes . . . Champaign, Ill., Flanigan–Pearson co., 1918. 2 p. l., 80 p.

University of Pennsylvania, 1918, PH. D.

Wendel, Hugo Christian Martin.

. . . The evolution of industrial freedom in Prussia, 1845–1849 . . . Allentown, Pa., H. R. Haas & co., 1918. 110 p.

University of Pennsylvania, 1918, PH. D.

Whaling, Heiskell Bryan.

. . . Fair value—economic and legal principles . . . Madison, Wis., 1918. 123 p.

(Bulletin of the University of Wisconsin, no. 923. Economics and political science series, v. 9. no. 3)
University of Wisconsin, 1915, PH. D.

Political Science

(Class J)

Boyce, Myrna M.

The diplomatic relations of England with the Quadruple alliance 1815–1830 . . . [Iowa City? 1918] 76 p.

University of Iowa, 1917, PH. D.
Published also as University of Iowa monographs, 1st ser., no. 22, November 1918.

Chang, Tso-Shuen.

History and analysis of the commission and city-manager plans of municipal government in the United States . . . Iowa City, Ia., 1918. 290 p.

Iowa university, 1917, PH. D.
Published also as University of Iowa monograph. 1st ser., no. 18, July, 1918. Studies in the social sciences, v. 1.

Dodds, Harold Willis, 1889–

.... Procedure in state legislatures ... Philadelphia, The American academy of political and social science, 1918. vi, 112 p.

University of Pennsylvania, 1917, PH. D.
Published also as Supplement no. 1 to the Annals of the American academy of political and social science, May, 1918.

Ellingwood, Albert Russell.

... Departmental coöperation in state government ... Menasha, Wis., George Banta publishing company, 1918. 6 p. l., 300 p.

University of Pennsylvania, 1918, PH. D.
Published also without thesis note.

Fox, Dixon Ryan, 1887–

The decline of aristocracy in the politics of New York ... New York, 1918. xiii, 460 p., 1 l.

Columbia university, 1917, PH. D.
Published also as Studies in history, economics and public law, ed. by the Faculty of political science of Columbia university, vol. LXXXVI, whole no. 198.

Garrett, Mitchell Bennett, 1881–

The French colonial question 1789–1791; dealings of the Constituent assembly with problems arising from the revolution in the West Indies ... Ann Arbor, Mich., G. Wahr ·[1918] iv p., 1 l., 167 p.

Cornell university, 1910, PH. D.
Published in 1916 without thesis note.

Hollingsworth, William Wiley.

... Woodrow Wilson's political ideals as interpreted from his works ... Princeton, Princeton university press, 1918. vi, 53 p.

University of Pennsylvania, 1918, PH. D.

Howell, Roger, 1895–

The privileges and immunities of state citizenship ... Baltimore, 1918. vii, 9–121 p.

Johns Hopkins university, 1917, PH. D.
Published also as Johns Hopkins university studies in historical and political science, ser. XXXVI, no. 3.

Lamprecht, Sterling Power, 1890–
The moral and political philosophy of John Locke . . .
New York, Columbia university press, 1918.   viii, 168 p., 1 l.

Columbia university, 1918, PH. D.
"Reprinted from Archives of philosophy, no. 11."

Moley, Raymond, 1886–
The state movement for efficiency and economy . . .
[New York? 1918]   2 p. l., iii–vi, 165 p.

Columbia university, 1918, PH. D.

Munro, Dana Gardner.
. . . The five republics of Central America; their political
and economic development and their relations with the
United States . . . New York [etc.] Oxford university press,
1918.   viii p., 1 l., 332 p.

University of Pennsylvania, 1917, PH. D.
Published also by the Carnegie endowment for international peace,
Division of economics and history.

Phinney, Chester Squire.
. . . Francis Lieber's influence on American thought
and some of his unpublished letters . . . Philadelphia,
International printing co., 1918.   85 p.

University of Pennsylvania, 1918, PH. D.

Porter, Kirk Harold.
. . . A history of suffrage in the United States . . .
Chicago, Ill., The University of Chicago press, 1918.   2 p. l.,
vii–xi, 260 p.

University of Chicago, 1918, PH. D.
Published also without thesis note.

Quigley, Harold Scott.
. . . The immunity of private property from capture at
sea . . . Madison, Wis., 1918.   200 p.

(Bulletin of the University of Wisconsin, no. 918. Economics and
political science series, v. 9, no. 2)
University of Wisconsin, 1916, PH. D.

Tai, En-Sai, 1894–
Treaty ports in China (a study in diplomacy) . . . New
York city [University printing office, Columbia university]
1918.   x, 202 p., 1 l.

Columbia university, 1918, PH. D.
Published also without thesis note.

Education

(Class L)

Alexander, Thomas, 1887–

The Prussian elementary schools . . . New York, The Macmillan company, 1918. viiip., 1 l., 571 p.

(*Lettered on cover:* Text-book series in education)
Columbia university, 1918, PH. D.
Thesis note attached to t.-p.

Beatty, Albert James, 1871–

A comparative study of corporation schools as to their organization, administration, and methods of instruction . . . [Urbana? 1918] 116 p.

University of Illinois, 1917, PH. D.

Brandenburg, George Clinton.

Psychological aspects of language . . . [Baltimore, 1918] cover-title, p. 313–332.

University of Wisconsin, 1915, PH. D.
Thesis note stamped on cover.
"Reprint from the Journal of educational psychology, vol. IX, no. 6, June, 1918."

Bridgman, Olga Louise, 1886– .

An experimental study of abnormal children, with special reference to the problems of dependency and delinquency . . . [Berkeley, 1918] cover-title, 59 p.

University of California, 1915, PH. D.
University of California publications in psychology, v. 3, no. 1, March 30, 1918, with a special thesis t.-p. dated May, 1915, attached to the cover-title.

Butterworth, Julian Edward.

. . . Problems in state high school finance . . . Yonkers-on-Hudson, N. Y., World book company, 1918. ix, 214 p.

(School efficiency monographs)
University of Iowa, 1911, PH. D.
Without thesis note.

Childs, Hubert Guy, 1871–

An investigation of certain phases of the reorganization movement in the grammar grades of Indiana public schools

. . . Fort Wayne, Ind., Fort Wayne printing co., 1918. viii, 187 p., 1 l.

Columbia university, 1918, PH. D.
Published also without thesis note.

Cornell, Clare Brown.

"A graduated scale for determining mental age" . . . [Frankfort, Ky., State journal co., 1918] 41 p.

University of Nebraska, 1915, PH. D.

Dushkin, Alexander Mordecai, 1890–

Jewish education in New York city . . . New York, The Bureau of Jewish education, 1918. 2 p. l., ix p., 1 l., 559 p., 1 l.

Columbia university, 1918, PH. D.

Engelhardt, Nickolaus Louis, 1882–

A school building program for cities . . . New York city, Teachers college, Columbia university, 1918. ix, 130 p., 1 l.

Columbia university, 1918, PH. D.
Published also as Contributions to education, Teachers college, Columbia university, no. 96.

Fukuya, Shoan Masuzo.

. . . An experimental study of attention from the standpoint of mental efficiency: a contribution to educational and social problems . . . [Princeton, Princeton university press, 1918] 3 p. l., 42 p.

University of Chicago, 1917, PH. D.
"Private edition distributed by the University of Chicago libraries, Chicago, Illinois."
"Reprinted from the Psychological monographs, vol. XXV, whole no. 110, 1918."

Good, Harry Gehman, 1880–

. . . Benjamin Rush and his services to American education . . . Berne, Ind., Witness press [1918] x, 283 p.

University of Pennsylvania, 1915, PH. D.
Published also without thesis note.

Gowin, Enoch Burton, 1883–

The selection and training of the business executive . . . New York, The Macmillan company, 1918. xii p., 1 l., 225 p.

Columbia university, 1918, PH. D.

Hobson, Elsie Garland.

. . . Educational legislation and administration in the state of New York, 1777–1850 . . . Chicago, Ill., 1918. 5 p. l., 267 p.

University of Chicago, 1916, PH. D.

"Private edition, distributed by the University of Chicago libraries."

Published also as Supplementary educational monographs, pub. in conjunction with the School review and the Elementary school journal, vol. III, no. 1, whole no. 11.

Hotz, Henry Gustave, 1880–

First year algebra scales . . . New York city, Teachers college, Columbia university, 1918. 3 p. l., 87, [1] p.

Columbia university, 1918, PH. D.

Ide, Gladys Genevra.

. . . The Witmer formboard and cylinders as tests for children two to six years of age . . . Philadelphia, Pa., The Psychological clinic press, 1918. 2 p. l., 24 p.

University of Pennsylvania, 1918, PH. D.

"Reprinted from the Psychological clinic, vol. XII, no. 3, May 15, 1918."

Kent, Raymond Asa, 1883–

A study of state aid to public schools in Minnesota . . . [Minneapolis] 1918. ix, 183, [1] p.

Columbia university, 1917, PH. D.

Published also as University of Minnesota Studies in the social sciences no. 11.

Kephart, Adam Perry, 1883–

. . . Clinical studies of failures with the Witmer formboard . . . Philadelphia, The Psychological clinic press, 1918. 1 p. l., p. 229–253.

University of Pennsylvania, 1918, PH. D.

"Reprinted from the Psychological clinic, vol. XI, no. 8, January, 1918."

Kruse, Paul Jehu, 1883–

The overlapping of attainments in certain sixth, seventh, and eighth grades . . . New York city, Teachers college, Columbia university, 1918. 3 p. l., 5–91, [1] p.

Columbia university, 1918, PH. D.

Published also as Contributions to education, Teachers college, Columbia university, no. 92.

Maddox, William Arthur, 1883–

The free school idea in Virginia before the civil war, a phase of political and social evolution . . . New York city, Teachers college, Columbia university, 1918. vi p., 1 l., 225 p., 1 l.

Columbia university, 1918, PH..D.
Published also as Contributions to education, Teachers college, Columbia university, no. 93.

Mateer, Florence.

Child behavior; a critical and experimental study of young children by the method of conditioned reflexes . . . Boston, R. G. Badger [1918] 2 p. l., 7–239 p.

Clark university, 1916, PH. D.
Published also without thesis note.

Mead, Arthur Raymond, 1880–

The development of free schools in the United States as illustrated by Connecticut and Michigan . . . New York city, Teachers college, Columbia university, 1918. 3 p. l., v–xi, 236 p., 1 l.

Columbia university, 1918, PH. D.
Published also as Contributions to education, Teachers college, Columbia university, no. 91.

Miller, Edward Alanson, 1866–

. . . The history of educational legislation in Ohio from 1803 to 1850 . . . [Columbus, 1918] 1 p. l., 286 p.

University of Chicago, 1915, PH. D.
"Private edition distributed by the University of Chicago libraries, Chicago, Illinois."
"Reprinted from Ohio archaeological and historical quarterly, volume XXVII, nos. 1 and 2, January and April, 1918."

Minnick, John Harrison, 1877–

. . . An investigation of certain abilities fundamental to the study of geometry . . . Lancaster, Pa., Press of the New era printing company, 1918. vii, 108 p.

University of Pennsylvania, 1918, PH. D.

Noble, Stuart Grayson, 1886–

Forty years of the public schools in Mississippi, with special reference to the education of the negro . . . New

York city, Teachers college, Columbia university, 1918.
iv p., 1 l., 142 p., 1 l.

Columbia university, 1918, PH. D.

Published also as Contributions to education, Teachers college, Columbia university, no. 94.

Paschal, Franklin Cressey, 1890–
. . . The Witmer cylinder test . . . Hershey, Pa., The Hershey press, 1918. 54 p.

University of Pennsylvania, 1918, PH. D.

Peters, Charles Clinton, 1887–
. . . Selection and organization of materials for a course in "the control of conduct" for secondary schools . . . Spring City, Pa., The Interborough press [1918]   120 p.

University of Pennsylvania, 1916, PH. D.

Robinson, Mabel Louise.
. . . The curriculum of the woman's college . . . Washington, Govt. print. off., 1918.   140 p.

([U. S.] Bureau of education. Bulletin, 1918, no. 6)
Columbia university, 1916, PH. D.
Slip with thesis note pasted on t.-p.

Roesch, *Sister* **Mary Jeanette,** 1884–
Vocational preparation of youth in Catholic schools . . . Washington, D. C., 1918.   73 p.

Catholic university of America, 1918, PH. D.

Rogers, Agnes Low, 1884–
Experimental tests of mathematical ability and their prognostic value . . . New York city, Teachers college, Columbia university, 1918.   v, 118 p., 1 l.

Columbia university, 1917, PH. D.
Published also as Teachers college, Columbia university. Contributions to education, no. 89.

Schuetz, John Joseph, 1874–
The origin of the teaching brotherhoods . . . Washington, D. C., 1918.   104 p.

Catholic university of America, 1918, PH. D.

Williams, Gertha, 1884–
. . . The problem of restoration; a clinical study . . . Menasha, Wis., George Banta publishing company, 1918. 2 p. l., 117 p.

University of Pennsylvania, 1917, PH. D.

Music

(Class M)

Armstrong, A. Joseph.

. . . Operatic performances in England before Handel . . . Waco, Tex. [Baylor university press] 1918. 74 p.

University of Pennsylvania, 1908, PH. D.
"Baylor university bulletin [vol. XXI] no. 4."

Hewitt, Theodore Brown.

Paul Gerhardt as a hymn writer and his influence on English hymnody . . . New Haven, Yale university press; [etc., etc.] 1918. xiv p., 1 l., 169 p.

"Presented to the Faculty of the Graduate school of Yale university in candidacy for the degree of doctor of philosophy in June, 1917."—Pref.

Wooley, Elmer Otto.

The sphere of music and musical terms in Goethe's lyric poems . . . Bloomington, Ind., 1918. 90 p.

Indiana university, 1915, PH. D.

Language and Literature

(Class P)

Amy, Ernest Francis, 1884–

The text of Chaucer's Legend of good women . . . Princeton, Princeton university press; [etc., etc.] 1918. ix, 109 p.

Princeton university, 1914, PH. D.

Baldwin, Thomas Whitfield, 1890–   *ed.*

An edition of Philip Massinger's Duke of Milan . . . by Thomas Whitfield Baldwin . . . Lancaster, Pa., Press of the New era printing company, 1918. ix, 197 p.

Princeton university, 1916, PH. D.
With reproduction of t.-p.: The Dvke of Millaine. A tragædie. As it hath beene often acted by his Maiesties seruants, at the blacke Friers. Written by Philip Massinger gent. London, Print<t>ed by B. A. for Edward Blackmore, 1623.

Beardslee, John Walter, 1879–
. . . The use of φύσις in fifth-century Greek literature . . . Chicago, Ill., The University of Chicago press, 1918. v, 126 p.

University of Chicago, 1913, PH. D.

Beckwith, Martha Warren, 1871–   *tr.*
The Hawaiian romance of Laieikawai with introduction and translation by Martha Warren Beckwith . . . Washington, Govt. print. off., 1918.   384 p.

Columbia university, 1918, PH. D.
Slip with thesis note mounted on t.-p.
"Translated from the Hawaiian text of S. N. Haleole (printed in Honolulu, 1863)"
"Reprinted from the Thirty-third annual report of the Bureau of American ethnology."

Blancké, Wilton Wallace.
. . . The dramatic values in Plautus . . . [Geneva, N. Y., Press of W. F. Humphrey] 1918.   69 p.

University of Pennsylvania, 1916, PH. D.

Bowen, Ray Preston, 1882–
The novels of Ferdinand Fabre, including an account of his life and a discussion of his position in literature . . . Boston, R. G. Badger [1918]   138 p., 1 l.

(*Half-title:* Studies in literature)
Cornell university, 1916, PH. D.
Published also without thesis note.

Brede, Charles Frederic.
. . . The German drama in English on the Philadelphia stage from 1794 to 1830 . . . Philadelphia, Americana Germanica press, 1918.   5 p. l., 3–295 p.

(*Half-title:* Americana Germanica. [no. 34])
University of Pennsylvania, 1905, PH. D.
Published also without thesis note.

Bruce, Harold Lawton, 1887–
. . . Voltaire on the English stage . . . Berkeley, University of California press [1918]   cover-title, p. [1]–152.

(University of California publications in modern philology. v. 8, no. 1)
"This study is the revision of a thesis of the same title submitted in 1915 to the Faculty of the Graduate school of Yale university in candidacy for the degree of doctor of philosophy."—Pref.

Campion, John Leo, 1884–

Das verwandtschaftsverhältnis der handschriften des Tristan Ulrichs von Türheim, nebst einer probe des kritischen textes . . . Baltimore, J. H. Furst company, 1918. 1 p. l., 42 p., 1 l.

Johns Hopkins university, 1917, PH. D.

Reprinted from Studies in philology, vol. xv, no. 1, January, 1918, p. 23–64.

Eller, William Henri.

Ibsen in Germany, 1870–1900 . . . Boston, R. G. Badger [°1918]   203 p.

(*Lettered on cover:* Studies in literature)

"The greater part of the following investigation was presented to the Graduate school at the University of Wisconsin, 1916, in partial fulfillment of the requirements for the degree of doctor of philosophy."—Pref.

Thesis note stamped on t.-p.

Ellinger, Esther Parker.

The southern war poetry of the civil war . . . Philadelphia, Pa. [Hershey, Pa., The Hershey press] 1918.   192 p.

University of Pennsylvania, 1918, PH. D.

Foster, Finley Melville Kendall, 1892–

English translations from the Greek; a bibliographical survey . . . New York, Columbia university press, 1918. xxix, 146 p., 1 l.

(*Half-title:* Columbia university studies in English and comparative literature)

Columbia university, 1918, PH. D.

Published also without thesis note.

Fundenburg, George Baer, 1893–

Feudal France in the French epic, a study of feudal French institutions in history and poetry . . . Princeton, N. J., 1918.   4 p. l., 121 p.

Columbia university, 1919, PH. D.

Goad, Caroline Mabel.

. . . Horace in the English literature of the eighteenth century . . . New Haven, Yale university press; [etc., etc.] 1918.   vi p., 1 l., 641 p.

(Yale studies in English, A. S. Cook, editor.   LVIII)

Yale university, 1916, PH. D.

Greene, William Chase.

Plato's view of poetry . . .

(*In* Harvard studies in classical philology. Cambridge, 1918. vol.
XXIX, p. 1–75)

"This essay in its original Latin form, entitled Quid de poetis Plato
censuerit, was presented in 1917 in partial fulfilment of the requirements
for the degree of doctor of philosophy in Harvard university."

Hamilton, Arthur, 1886–

Sources of the religious element in Flaubert's Salammbô
. . Baltimore, The Johns Hopkins press, 1918. 1 p. l.,
32 p., 1 l.

Johns Hopkins university, 1914, PH. D.
"An incomplete reprint from the Elliott monographs, no. 4."

Harmon, Esther, 1880–

Johanna Schopenhauer . . . München, Kgl. hofbuchdr.
Kastner & Callwey, 1914. 115 p., 1 l.

. Bryn Mawr college, 1912, PH. D.
"Ein abschnitt derselben unter dem titel 'Johanna Schopenhauer als
schriftstellerin' erschien 1910 in dem 'Journal of English and Germanic
philology,' vol. 9, nr. 2, 1910."

Harris, Lynn Harold, *ed.*

. . . Catiline his conspiracy, by Ben Jonson, ed., with
introduction, notes and glossary, by Lynn Harold Harris
. . . New Haven, Yale university press; [etc., etc.] 1916.
lxi, 236 p.

(Yale studies in English, A. S. Cook, editor. LIII)
Yale university, 1914, PH. D.
With reproduction of original t.-p.

Harvitt, Hélène Josephine, 1884–

Eustorg de Beaulieu, a disciple of Marot, 1495 (?)–1552
. . . Lancaster, Pa., Press of the New era printing company, 1918. ix, 164 p.

Columbia university, 1913, PH. D.
"Reprinted from the Romanic review, vol. V, no. 3 (1914), pp. 252–275;
vol. VI, no. 1 (1915), pp. 42–59; no. 2, pp. 206–218; no. 3, pp. 298–326; vol.
VII, no. 1 (1916), pp. 83–109; vol. IX, no. 3 (1918), pp. 319–344."

Hays, Heber Michel.

. . . Notes on the Works and days of Hesiod, with
introduction and appendix . . . Chicago, Ill., 1918. 2 p. l.,
226 p.

University of Chicago, 1915, PH. D.
"Private edition, distributed by the University of Chicago libraries."

Heider, Andrew Bernard, 1880–
The blessed Virgin Mary in early Christian Latin poetry
. . . Washington, D. C., 1918.   79, [1] p.

Catholic university of America, 1918, PH. D.

Henderson, Walter Brooks Drayton.
Swinburne and Landor, a study of their spiritual relationship and its effect on Swinburne's moral and poetic
development . . . London, Macmillan and co., limited,
1918.   viii, 304 p.

"The better part of this essay, together with its appendices, was submitted to the Faculty of Princeton university in partial fulfilment of the
requirement for the degree of doctor of philosophy in English literature,
in 1915."—Pref.

Holtzhausser, Clara A.
. . . An epigraphic commentary on Suetonius's life of
Tiberius . . . Philadelphia, Pa., 1918.   47 p.

University of Pennsylvania, 1918, PH. D.

House, Roy Temple, 1878– ed.
. . . L'Ordene de chevalerie; an old French poem, text,
with introduction and notes . . . by Roy Temple House
. . . Chicago, Ill., 1918.   2 p. l., 69 p.

University of Chicago, 1917, PH. D.
"Private edition, distributed by the University of Chicago libraries."

Jacob, Cary Franklin, 1885–
The foundations and nature of verse . . . New York,
Columbia university press, 1918.   ix p., 1 l., 231 p., 1 l.

University of Virginia, 1917, PH. D.
Published also without thesis note.

Le Duc, Alma de Lande, 1878–
Gontier Col and the French pre-renaissance . . . New
York, 1918.   vii, 103, [1] p.

Columbia university, 1916, PH. D.
"Reprinted from the Romanic review, vol. VII, no. 4, 414–457, 1916; vol.
VIII, no. 2, 145–165, and no. 3, 290–306, 1917."

Leffingwell, Georgia Williams, 1893–
Social and private life at Rome in the time of Plautus
and Terence . . . New York, 1918.   2 p. l., 7–141 p.

Columbia university, 1918, PH. D.
Published also as Studies in history, economics and public law, edited
by the Faculty of political science of Columbia university.   vol. LXXXI, no.
1; whole no. 188.

Lockert, Charles Lacy, 1888–   *ed.* .

The fatal dowry, by Philip Massinger and Nathaniel Field, ed., from the original quarto, with introduction and notes . . . by Charles Lacy Lockert, jr. . . . Lancaster, Pa., Press of the New era printing company, 1918.   iii, 167 p.

Princeton university, 1916, PH. D.

Messer, William Stuart, 1882–

The dream in Homer and Greek tragedy . . .   New York, Columbia university press, 1918.   viii p., 1 l., 105, [1] p.

(*Half-title:* Columbia university studies in classical philology)
Columbia university, 1918, PH. D.
Published also without thesis note.

Michel, Virgil G., 1890–

The critical principles of Orestes A. Brownson . . . Washington, D. C., 1918.   106 p., 1 l.

Catholic university of America,   , PH. D.

Moore, Charlotte.

. . . The dramatic works of Thomas Nabbes . . .   Part I. Menasha, Wis., George Banta publishing company, 1918. 3 p. l., 61, [1] p.

University of Pennsylvania, 1915, PH. D.
"Part II of this thesis consists of a transcript of the quarto text, 1637, of Hannibal and Scipio, with some introductory pages remaining from the part here published.   The text is accompanied with notes and a glossary."

Norlie, Olaf Morgan, 1876–

Principles of expressive reading, impression before expression . . .   Boston, The Gorham press, 1918.   2 p. l., 3–190 p.

University of Minnesota, 1908, PH. D.
Thesis note is Note 1 on p. 165.

Pasmore, Daniel Frederick, 1889–

Karl Gutzkow's short stories, a study in the technique of narration . . .   [Urbana? 1918]   4 p. l., 122 p., 1 l.

University of Illinois, 1917, PH. D.

Quimby, Mary Agnes.

. . . The nature background in the dramas of Gerhart Hauptmann . . .   Philadelphia, International printing company, 1918.   68 p.

University of Pennsylvania, 1918, PH. D.
33564°—21——9

Rowland, William Tingle, 1881–

On the position in the clause of *ne* and *ut* in certain documents of colloquial Latin . . . New York, Columbia university press, 1918. 4 p. l., 44 p., 1 l.

(*Half-title:* Columbia university studies in classical philology)
Columbia university,   , PH. D.
Published also without thesis note.

Schaffer, Aaron, 1894–

Georg Rudolf Weckherlin, the embodiment of a transitional stage in German metrics. Chapter I. German metrics from earliest times to Opitz . . . Baltimore, J. H. Furst company, 1918. 3 p. l., 57 p., 1 l.

Johns Hopkins university, 1917, PH. D.
"The complete monograph will be issued as number 10 of 'Hesperia: Studies in Germanic philology,' edited by Profs. Hermann Collitz and Henry Wood."

Scholz, Karl William Henry, 1887–

. . . The art of translation, with special reference to English renditions of the prose dramas of Gerhart Hauptmann and Hermann Sudermann . . . Philadelphia, Pa., 1918. 5 p. l., 3–70 p.

(*Half-title:* Americana germanica. [no. 33])
University of Pennsylvania, 1918, PH. D.
Published also without thesis note.

Sell, Lewis Lazarus, 1890–

De Catvlli carmine sexagesimo qvarto qvaestiones diversae . . . Novi Eboraci, ex officina W. D. Gray, 1918. 2 p. l., 110 p., 1 l.

Columbia university, 1918, PH. D.

Shafer, Samuel Robert, 1890–

The English ode to 1660; an essay in literary history . . . Princeton, Princeton university press; [etc., etc.] 1918. vi, 167 p.

Princeton university, 1916, PH. D.

Slaten, Arthur Wakefield.

. . . Qualitative nouns in the Pauline Epistles and their translation in the revised version . . . Chicago, Ill., The University of Chicago press, 1918. 1 p. l., v–vii, 70 p.

University of Chicago, 1916, PH. D.
"Historical and linguistic studies, second series, vol. IV, part I."

Snell, Ada Laura Fonda, 1871–
. . . Pause; a study of its nature and its rhythmical function in verse, especially blank verse . . . Ann Arbor [The Ann Arbor press] 1918. 2 p. l., 85, [1] p.

(Contributions to rhetorical theory, ed. by F. N. Scott . . . VIII)
University of Michigan, 1916, PH. D.

Snyder, Alice Dorothea, 1887–
. . . The critical principle of the reconciliation of opposites as employed by Coleridge . . . Ann Arbor [The Ann Arbor press] 1918. 3 p. l., 59 p.

(Contributions to rhetorical theory, ed. by F. N. Scott . . . IX)
University of Michigan, 1915, PH. D.
Published also without thesis note.

Spring, Evelyn.
A study of exposition in Greek tragedy . . . [Boston, 1917] 1 p. l., p. 135–224.

"This essay in its original form, entitled Quo modo Aeschylus in tragoediis suis res antecedentis exposuerit, was presented in 1915 in partial fulfilment of the requirements for the degree of doctor of philosophy in Radcliffe college."
"Printed from the Harvard studies in classical philology, vol. XXVIII, 1917."

Swann, Harvey Julian, 1884–
French terminologies in the making; studies in conscious contributions to the vocabulary . . . New York, Columbia university press, 1918. xxii, 250 p., 1 l.

(*Half-title:* Columbia university studies in Romance philology and literature)
Columbia university, 1918, PH. D.
Published also without thesis note.

Taylor, John Prentice.
The mythology of Vergil's Aeneid according to Servius . . . [New York, 1918] 4 p. l., 62 p.

New York university, 1917, PH. D.

Vaeth, Joseph Anthony, 1876–
Tirant lo Blanch; a study of its authorship, principal sources and historical setting . . . New York, Columbia university press, 1918. xvi, 169 p., 1 l.

(*Half-title:* Columbia university studies in Romance philology and literature)
Columbia university, 1917, PH. D.
Published also without thesis note.

Vollmer, Clement.
. . . The American novel in Germany, 1871–1913 . . .
Philadelphia, International printing co., 1918. 3 p. l, [9]–94 p.
University of Pennsylvania, 1915, PH. D.

Wann, Louis.
The Oriental in Elizabethan drama . . . [Chicago, 1915]
cover-title, p. 163–187.
University of Wisconsin, 1919, PH. D.
Part I of thesis.
Thesis note stamped on cover of pt. I.
"Reprinted for private circulation from Modern philology, vol. XII,
no. 7, January, 1915."

Wann, Louis.
The Oriental in restoration drama . . . [Madison, Wis.,
1918] cover-title, p. [163]–186.
University of Wisconsin, 1919, PH. D.
Part II of thesis.
"Reprinted from University of Wisconsin studies in language and liter-
ature number 2."

Wooley, Elmer Otto.
The sphere of music and musical terms in Goethe's lyric
poems . . . Bloomington, Ind., 1918. 90 p.
Indiana university, 1915, PH. D.

Zeydel, Edwin Hermann, 1893–
The Holy Roman empire in German literature . . . New
York, Columbia university press, 1918. ix, 144 p.
(*Half-title:* Columbia university Germanic studies)
Columbia university, 1918, PH. D.
Published also without thesis note.

Science

(Class Q)

Abbott, Raymond Barrington, 1873–
Law of motion of a droplet moving with variable velocity in air . . . Lancaster, Pa., Press of the New era printing
company [1918] 1 p. l., p. [381]–395.
University of California, 1919, PH. D.
"Reprinted from the Physical review, n. s., vol. XII, no. 5, November,
1918."

Adamson, William Augustus, 1883–

2, 4-dihydroxybenzoyltetrachloro-o-benzoic acid and 2, 3, 4-trichloro-6-hydroxyxanthone-1-carboxylic acid and some of their derivatives, by W. R. Orndorff and W. A. Adamson . . . [Easton, Pa., 1918] 1 p. l., p. [1235]–1257·

"A reprint of an article based upon a thesis submitted to the Faculty of the Graduate school of Cornell university for the degree of doctor of philosophy, by William Augustus Adamson, 1917."

W. R. Orndorff, instructor under whom thesis was written.

"Reprinted from the Journal of the American chemical society, vol. XL, no. 8. August, 1918."

Adkins, Homer Burton, 1892–

The oxidation by means of alkaline potassium permanganate of acetaldehyde glycol, glycollic aldehyde, glyoxal, glycollic and glyoxalic acids . . . Columbus, O., 1918. 32p.

Ohio state university, 1918, PH. D.

Aronberg, Lester.

. . . Note on the spectrum of the isotopes of lead. The structure of the bismuth line 4722 . . . [Chicago, 1918] 1 p. l., p. 96–103.

University of Chicago, 1917, PH. D.

"Private edition, distributed by the University of Chicago libraries, Chicago, Illinois."

"Reprinted from the Astrophysical journal, vol. XLVII, no. 2, March, 1918."

Artschwager, Ernst Friedrich, 1889–

Anatomy of the potato plant, with special reference to the ontogeny of the vascular system . . . [Washington, D. C., 1918] 1 p. l., p. 221–252.

Cornell university, 1918, PH. D.

"Reprinted from Journal of agricultural research, vol. XIV, no. 6, Washington, D. C., August 5, 1918."

Atwell, Wayne Jason, 1889–

The development of the hypophysis cerebri of the rabbit (*Lepus cuniculus* L.) . . . Philadelphia [1918] 1 p. l., p. 271–337.

University of Michigan, 1917, PH. D.

"Reprinted from the American journal of anatomy, vol. 24, no. 3, September, 1918."

"Author's abstract of this paper issued by the [Wistar institute] Bibliographic service, July 19."

Bakke, Arthur Laurence.

. . . Determination of wilting . . . [Chicago, 1918] 1 p. l., p. 81–116.

University of Chicago, 1917, PH. D.
"Private edition, distributed by the University of Chicago libraries, Chicago, Illinois."
"Reprinted from the Botanical gazette, vol. LXVI, no. 2, August, 1918."
"Contributions from the Hull botanical laboratory 241."

Baldwin, Francis Marsh, 1885–

Pharyngeal derivatives of *Amblystoma* . . . Philadelphia, 1918. 1 p. l., 605–680 p., 1 l.

University of Illinois, 1917, PH. D.
"Author's abstract of this paper issued by the [Wistar institute] Bibliographic service, March 2."
"Contributions from the Zoological laboratories of the University of Illinois no. 103."
"Reprinted from the Journal of morphology, vol. 30, no. 2, March, 1918."

Barrows, Albert Lloyd, 1883–

The significance of the skeletal variations in the genus *Peridinium* . . . [Berkeley, 1918] cover-title, [397]–478, [1] p.

University of California, 1917, PH. D.
University of California publications in zoology, v. 18, no. 15, June 27, 1918, with a special thesis t.-p. dated May 1917 attached to the cover-title.

Bast, Victor August, 1883–

The action of calcium carbide on benzaldehyde and on some other organic compounds . . . [Washington, D. C.] Catholic university of America, 1918. 93 p.

Catholic university of America, 1918, PH. D.

Beckerman, Harry.

. . . I. Tungsten hexabromide. II. Tungsten complexes . . . Philadelphia, Pa., 1918. 19 p.

University of Pennsylvania, 1918, PH. D.

Beegle, Frank Moore, 1889–

A study of the mutarotation of glucose and fructose . . . New York, 1918. 21, [1] p.

Columbia university, 1918, PH. D.

Behre, Ellinor Helene.

. . . An experimental study of acclimation to temperature in *Planaria dorotocephala* . . . [Lancaster, Pa., Press of the New era printing company, 1918] 1 p. l., p. 277–317.

University of Chicago, 1918, PH. D.

"Private edition, distributed by the University of Chicago libraries, Chicago, Illinois."

"Reprinted from Biological bulletin, vol. xxxv., no. 5, November, 1918."

Bichowsky, Francis Russell von.

Equilibrium in the reaction between water and sulfur at high temperatures. The dissociation of hydrogen sulfide . . . [Easton, Pa., 1918] cover-title, p. [368]–375.

University of California, 1916, PH. D.

Thesis t.-p. attached to cover of the issue, by Merle Randall and F. Russell v. Bichowsky, which was reprinted from the Journal of the American chemical society, vol. XL, no. 2, February, 1918.

Blanchard, Julian, 1885–

The brightness sensibility of the retina . . . Lancaster, Pa., Press of the New era printing company, 1918. 1 p. l., 81–99, [1] p.

Columbia university, 1917, PH. D.

"Reprinted from the Physical review, vol. XI, no. 2, February, 1918."

"Communication no. 45 from the research laboratory of the Eastman kodak company."

Blumberg, Alfred.

Studies in immunity with special reference to complement fixation . . . Washington, D. C. [1918] cover-title, 11, [1] p.

George Washington university, 1917, PH. D.

"Reprint from the Journal of laboratory and clinical medicine, vol. III, no. 7, April, 1918."

Bock, Carl William, 1888–

The association of voluntary movements . . . [Baltimore, 1918] 1 p. l., p. 277–318, 1 l.

Ohio state university, 1917, PH. D.

"Reprinted from Psychobiology, vol. I, no. 4, January, 1918."

Bonns, Walter Weidenfeld, 1877–
. . . Etherization of tissues and its effect on enzyme activity . . . [St. Louis, 1918] cover-title, p. 225–299.

(Washington university doctoral dissertations)
Washington university, St. Louis, 1918, PH. D.
"Publications of Washington university, Saint Louis, series v, number 29."
"Reprinted from Annals of the Missouri botanical garden, November, 1918, vol. v, no. 4."

Bovard, John Freeman, 1881–
The transmission of nervous impulses in relation to locomotion in the earthworm . . . [Berkeley, 1918] 2 pt.

University of California, 1917, PH. D.
University of California publications in zoology, v. 18, nos. 7, 8, with a special thesis t.-p. dated May, 1917 attached to the cover-title of [pt. 1]
[Pt. 2] has title: The function of the giant fibers in earthworms.

Bowman, Howard Hiestand Minnich, 1886–
Ecology and physiology of the red mangrove . . . Philadelphia, 1918. 1 p. l., p. [589]–673.

University of Pennsylvania, 1917, PH. D.
"Reprinted from Proceedings American philosophical society, vol. LVI, 1917."

Bramble, Charles Clinton, 1890–
A collineation group isomorphic with the group of the double tangents of the plant quartic . . '. [Baltimore, 1918] 1 p. l., [351]–365 p., 1 l.

Johns Hopkins university, 1917, PH. D.
"Reprinted from American journal of mathematics, vol. XL, no. 4, October, 1918."

Bridgman, J. Allington, 1892–
Gallium . . . [Easton, Pa., 1918] 33 p.

. Cornell university, 1917, PH. D.
"Reprinted from the Journal of the American chemical society, vol. XL, no. 10, October, 1918."

Brighton, Thomas Bow, 1887–
The free energy of formation of cyanide ion and of hydrocyanic acid . . . [Easton, Pa., 1918] cover-title, p. [482]–489.

University of California, 1917, PH. D.
Thesis t.-p. attached to the cover of the reprint from the Journal of the American chemical society, vol. XL, no. 3, March 1918, which has title: The oxidizing power of cyanates and the free energy of formation of cyanides, by Gilbert N. Lewis and Thomas B. Brighton.

Brockbank, Thomas William.

Redintegration in the albino rat, a study in retention . . . Washington, D. C., 1918.   2 p. l., 66 p.

Catholic university of America, 1918, PH. D.
Published also as Behavior monographs, v. 4, no. 2, serial no. 18.

Broderick, Thomas M.

The relation of the titaniferous magnetite deposits of northeastern Minnesota to the Duluth gabbro . . . Lancaster, Pa., Press of the New era printing company, 1918. 1 p. l., p. 663–696, 35–49.

University of Minnesota, 1917, PH. D.
Reprinted from Economic geology, vol. XII, no. 8, December, 1917; vol. XIII, no. 1, January, 1918.

Brown, Thomas Benjamin, 1892–

Kathodo-fluorescence of crystals, by Thomas B. Brown. Part I.—A quantitative investigation of the kathodo-fluorescence of willemite, kunzite, and soda glass. (A description of the results obtained by J. A. Veazey.) Part II.—A further investigation of willemite by the writer . . . Lancaster, Pa., Press of the New era printing company, 1918.   1 p. l., p. [39]–57.

"Part I is the substance of a thesis presented to the Faculty of the Graduate school of Cornell university by J. A. Veazey for the degree of doctor of philosophy."

"Part II is a thesis presented to the Faculty of the Graduate school of Cornell university by Thomas B. Brown for the degree of doctor of philosophy." 1916.

"Since the untimely death of J. A. Veazey prevented the immediate publication of his thesis, and since the work of the writer is so closely related to this previous work, these two papers are here issued as a single publication."

"Reprinted from Physical review, vol. XI, no. 1, January, 1918."

Buchholz, John Theodore.

. . . Suspensor and early embryo of *Pinus* . . . [Chicago, 1918] 1 p. l., p. 185–228.

University of Chicago, 1917, PH. D.
"Private edition, distributed by the University of Chicago libraries, Chicago, Illinois."

"Reprinted from the Botanical gazette, vol. LXVI, no. 3, September 1918."

"Contributions from the Hull botanical laboratory 242."

Burwash, Edward Moore Jackson, 1873–
. . . The geology of Vancouver and vicinity . . . Chicago, Ill., The University of Chicago press, 1918. 3 p. l., 3–106 p.

University of Chicago, 1915, PH. D.

Chapman, Royal Norton, 1889–
The basal connections of the tracheae of the wings of insects . . . Ithaca, N. Y., The Comstock publishing company, 1918. 1 p. l., p. 27–51.

Cornell university, 1917, PH. D.
"Reprinted from The wings of insects by John Henry Comstock."

Clark, Guy Wendell, 1887–
The properties and composition of oocytin . . . [Baltimore, The Waverly press] 1918. cover-title, p. 253–262.

University of California, 1918, PH. D.
Reprint from the Journal of biological chemistry, vol. XXXV, no. 2, August 1918, with a special thesis t.-p. dated June, 1918, attached to the cover-title.

Cohn, Edwin Joseph.
. . . Studies in the physiology of spermatozoa . . . [Lancaster, Pa., 1918] 1 p. l., p. 167–218.

University of Chicago, 1917, PH. D.
"Private edition, distributed by the University of Chicago libraries, Chicago, Illinois."
"Reprinted from Biological bulletin, vol. XXXIV, no. 3, March 1918."

Cole, Howard Irving, 1892–
The use of textile fibers in microscopic qualitative chemical analysis . . . [Easton, Pa., 1917–18] 1 p. l., 7, 7 p.

Cornell university, 1917, PH. D.
"Reprinted from the Journal of industrial and engineering chemistry, vol. 9, no. 10, page 969. October, 1917; vol. 10, no. 1, page 48. January, 1918."

Coombs, Helen Copeland, 1891–
The relation of the dorsal roots of the spinal nerves and the mesencephalon to the control of the respiratory movements . . . [Boston, 1918] 1 p. l., p. 459–471, 1 l.

Columbia university, 1918, PH. D.
"Reprinted from the American journal of physiology, vol. XLVI, July, 1918."

Cornell, Ethel Letitia, 1892–

A new clinical test for temperature sensitivity, a contribution to the study of temperature reaction in nervous diseases based on the reaction to simultaneous cold and hot stimulation . . . New York, P. B. Hoeber, 1918. 1 p. l., 119–158, 335–372 p., 1 l.

Columbia university, 1919, PH. D.
"Reprinted from vol. I, no. 3 . . . and vol. I, no. 9 . . . The Neurological bulletin . . . °1918."

Crooker, Sylvan Jay, 1893–

. . . Influence of a series spark on the direct current corona . . . [New Haven, 1918] 1 p. l., p. 281–300, 1 l.

University of Illinois, 1917, PH. D.
"Reprinted from the American journal of science, vol. XLV, April, 1918."

Curtis, George Morris, 1890–

The morphology of the mammalian seminiferous tubule . . . Philadelphia [1918] 1 p. l., p. 339–394.

University of Michigan, 1914, PH. D.
"Reprinted from the American journal of anatomy, vol. 24, no. 3, September, 1918."
"Author's abstract of this paper issued by the [Wistar institute] Bibliographic service, July 19."

Curtis, Otis Freeman, 1888–

Stimulation of root growth in cuttings by treatment with chemical compounds . . . [Ithaca, 1918] 1 p. l., p. 71–138.

Cornell university, 1916, PH. D.
"Reprinted from Memoir no. 14, August, 1918, of Cornell university agricultural experiment station."

Davidson, Joseph George, 1892–

The formation of aromatic hydrocarbons from natural gas condensate . . . New York city, 1918. 37, [1] p.

Columbia university, 1918, PH. D.

Davis, Elmer Fred, 1887–

Rocks of the Franciscan group. 1. The sandstone. 2. The radiolarian cherts . . . [Berkeley, 1918] 2 pt.

University of California, 1917, PH. D.
University of California publications, Bulletin of the Department of geology, v. 11, nos. 1 and 3, with a special thesis t.-p. attached to the cover of [pt. 1]

Dawson, Andrew Ignatius, 1876–
Variations in bacteria caused by change of medium . . . [New York?] 1918.   2 p. l., 15, [1] p.

Columbia university, 1918, PH. D.

De Porte, Joseph Vital, 1889–
Irrational involutions on algebraic curves . . .   [Baltimore, 1918]   1 p. l., p. [47]–68.

Cornell university, 1916, PH. D.
"Reprinted from American journal of mathematics, vol. XL, no. 1, January, 1918."

Derieux, John Bewley.
. . . The use of mercury drops in Millikan's experiment. Photoelectric effects on mercury droplets . . .   [Lancaster, Pa., and Ithaca, N. Y., 1918]   1 p. l., [203]–226, [1], [276]–284 p.

University of Chicago, 1919, PH. D.
"Private edition, distributed by the University of Chicago libraries, Chicago, Illinois."
"Reprinted from the Physical review, n. s., vol. XI, nos. 3 and 4, March and April, 1918."

Dodson, John Dillingham.
An experimental study of the relative values of reward and punishment in habit formation . . .   [Baltimore, 1917] cover-title, p. 231–276.

University of Minnesota, 1918, PH. D.
On cover: Department of psychology, April, 1918.
"Reprinted from Psychobiology, vol. I, no. 3, November, 1917."

Douglas, Gertrude Elizabeth, 1883–
A study of development in the family *Agaricaceae*.   Part I: A study of development in the genus *Cortinarius*.   Part II: The development of some exogenous species of agarics . . . [Lancaster, Pa., 1916–18]   1 p. l., p. 319–335, [35]–54.

Cornell university, 1917, PH.. D.
"Reprinted from Am. jour. bot., vol. 3: June 1916 . . . vol. 5: Jan. 1918."

Dudgeon, Winfield Scott.
. . . Morphology of *Rumex crispus* . . .   [Chicago, 1918] 1 p. l., p. 393–420.

University of Chicago, 1917, PH. D.

"Private edition, distributed by the University of Chicago libraries, Chicago, Illinois."

"Reprinted from the Botanical gazette, vol. LXVI, no. 5, November, 1918."

"Contributions from the Hull botanical laboratory 244."

Dunbar, Carl Owen.

. . . Stratigraphy and correlation of the Devonian of western Tennessee . . . . [New Haven, 1918] cover-title, p. 732–756.

Yale university, 1917, PH. D.

Abstract of thesis.

"Contributions from the Paleontological laboratory, Peabody museum, Yale university, New Haven, Conn., U. S. A."

"From the American journal of science, vol. XLVI, December, 1918."

Eastman, Ermon Dwight, 1891–

The measurement of low temperatures and the measurement of specific heats between 60 degrees and 300 degrees absolute . . . [Easton, Pa., 1918] cover-title, p. [489]–500.

University of California, 1917, PH. D.

Thesis t.-p. attached to the cover of the reprint from the Journal of the American chemical society, vol. XL, no. 3, March, 1918, which has title: The specific heats at low temperatures of sodium, potassium, magnesium and calcium metals, and of lead sulfide, by E. D. Eastman and W. H. Rodebush.

Eberson, Frederick, 1892–

A bacteriologic study of the diphtheroid organisms with special reference to Hodgkin's disease . . . New York city, 1918. 56 p.

Columbia university, 1918, PH. D.

Essenberg, Christine Elizabeth, 1879–

The factors controlling the distribution of the *Polynoidae* of the Pacific coast of North America . . . [Berkeley, 1918] cover-title, p. [171]–238.

University of California, 1917, PH. D.

University of California publications in zoology, v. 18, no. 11, March 8, 1918, with a special thesis t.-p. dated May, 1917, attached to the cover-title.

Faust, Ernest Carroll, 1890–

Life history studies on Montana trematodes . . . [Urbana, 1918] 120 p., 1 l.

University of Illinois, 1917, PH. D.

"Reprinted from the Illinois biological monographs, vol. 4: 1–120."

Felsing, William August, 1891-

I. The equilibrium of the reaction $Ag_2S + H_2 = 2Ag + H_2S$.
II. The equation of state of ether vapor . . . [Cambridge, Mass.] Technology press, 1918. 39 p.

Massachusetts institute of technology, 1918, PH. D.
Abstract of thesis.

Fenton, Frederick Azel, 1893-

The parasites of leaf-hoppers, with special reference to biology of the *Anteoninae* . . . [Columbus, O.] 1918. cover-title, [84] p.

(Ohio state university. Contributions from the Department of zoology and entomology. no. 51)
Ohio state university, 1918, PH. D.
Without thesis note.
Reprinted from the Ohio journal of science, vol. XVIII, no. 6, p. 177–212; no. 7, p. 243–278; no. 8, p. 285–296.

Folsom, Donald.

The influence of certain environmental conditions, especially water supply, upon form and structure in *Ranunculus* . . . [Baltimore, 1918] 1 p. l., p. 209–276.

University of Minnesota, 1917, PH. D.
"Reprinted from Physiological researches. vol. 2, no. 5, December, 1918."

Foote, Paul Darwin, 1888-

Some characteristics of the Marvin pyrheliometer . . . [Washington, 1918] cover-title, 1 p. l., p. 605–634.

University of Minnesota, 1917, PH. D.
Issued also as Scientific papers no. 323 of the Bureau of standards. This issue is identical with that, with the addition of a cover-title.

Freas, Raymond, 1886-

Esterification limits of benzoic and toluic acids with lower alcohols . . . Easton, Pa., Eschenbach printing co., 1918. 14 p., 1 l.

Johns Hopkins university, 1917, PH. D.

Freed, Edgar Stanley, 1899-

1. A thermodynamic investigation of reactions involving silver sulfide and silver iodide. II. The equilibrium between nitric oxide, nitrogen, peroxide, and aqueous solutions of nitric acid . . . [Cambridge, Mass.] Technology press, 1918. 16 p.

Massachusetts institute of technology, 1918, PH. D.
Abstract of thesis.

Friedline, Cora Louisa, 1893–
The discrimination of cutaneous patterns below the two-point limen . . . [Worcester, 1918] 1 p. l., p. 400–419.

Cornell university, 1918, PH. D.
"Reprinted from the American journal of psychology, October, 1918, vol. XXIX."

Fulmer, Henry Luman, 1888–
Influence of carbonates of magnesium and calcium on bacteria of certain Wisconsin soils . . . Washington, Govt. print. off., 1918. cover-title, p. 463–504.

University of Wisconsin, 1917, PH. D.
Thesis note stamped on cover.
"Reprinted from Journal of agricultural research, vol. XII, no. 8 . . . February 25, 1918."

Furman, Nathaniel Howell, 1892–
The use of hydrofluoric acid in analysis and The behavior of solutions of stannic fluoride. . . . [Easton, Pa., Eschenbach printing co., 1918] 23 p.

Princeton university, 1917, PH. D.

Gaehr, Paul Frederick, 1880–
The specific heat of tungsten at incandescent temperatures . . . Lancaster, Pa., Press of the New era printing company [1918] [1], [396]–423 p.

Cornell university, 1918, PH. D.
"Reprinted from the Physical review, vol. XII, no. 5, November, 1918."

Garretson, William Van Nest, 1879–
On the asymptotic solution of the non-homogeneous linear differential equation of the n-th order. A particular solution . . . [Baltimore, 1918] 1 p. l., p. [341]–350.

University of Michigan, 1916, PH. D.
"Reprinted from American journal of mathematics, vol. XL, no. 4, October, 1918.".

Gordon, Newell Trimble, 1891–
Potential measurements on the copper-nickel series of alloys, and some observations on brasses . . . Easton, Pa., Eschenbach printing company, 1918. cover-title, 24 p.

Princeton university, 1919, PH. D.

Goudge, Mabel Ensworth, 1885–

A qualitative and quantitative study of Weber's illusion . . . [Worcester, Mass., 1918] 1 p. l., p. 81–119.

Cornell university, 1914, PH. D.

"Reprinted from the American journal of psychology, January, 1918, vol. XXIX."

Grant, Elmer Daniel, 1873–

. . . Motion of a flexible cable in a vertical plane . . . [Lancaster, Pa., Press of the New era printing company] 1918. 1 p. l., 28 p.

University of Chicago, 1916, PH. D.

"Private edition, distributed by the University of Chicago libraries, Chicago, Illinois."

Grout, Frank Fitch, 1880–

The Duluth gabbro and its associated formations . . . [New Haven? 1918] 6 pt. in 1 v.

Yale university, 1917, PH..D.

"A set of articles arranged for publication from a dissertation."

[pt. 1] Economic geology, vol. XIII, no. 3, May, 1918—[pt. 2] American journal of science, vol. XLVI, Sept., 1918—[pt. 3] Journal of geology, vol. XXVI, no. 5, July–August, 1918—[pt. 4] Journal of geology, vol. XXVI, no. 6, Sept.–Oct., 1918—[pt. 5] Journal of geology, vol. XXVI, no. 7, Oct.–Nov., 1918 [pt. 6] Journal of geology, vol. XXVI, no. 7, Oct.–Nov., 1918.

Hanke, Milton Theodore.

. . . The oxidation of maltose in alkaline solution by hydrogen peroxide and by air, the preparation and study of maltobionic acid . . . Chicago, Ill., 1918. 3 p. l., 36 p.

University of Chicago, 1917, PH. D.

"Private edition, distributed by the University of Chicago libraries."

Harding, Earle Atherton, 1887–

A study of the occlusion of hydrogen and oxygen by metal electrodes . . . Easton, Pa., Eschenbach printing co., 1918. 2 p. l., [3]–26 p.

Princeton university, 1918, PH. D.

Harvey, Rodney Beecher, 1890–

. . . Hardening process in plants and developments from frost injury . . . [Washington, 1918] 1 p. l., p. 83–112.

University of Chicago, 1918, PH. D.

"Private edition, distributed by the University of Chicago libraries, Chicago, Illinois."

"Reprinted from the Journal of agricultural research, vol. XV, no. 2, October, 1918."

Haseman, Mary Gertrude, 1889–

On knots, with a census of the amphicheirals with twelve crossings . . . Edinburgh, Printed by Neill & co., limited, 1918. 1 p. l., p. [235]–255.

Bryn Mawr college, 1918, PH. D.
"Reprinted from the Transactions of the Royal society of Edinburgh, vol. LII, 1917."

Hebbert, Clarence Mark, 1890–

Some circular curves generated by pencils of stelloids and their polars . . . [Urbana, 1918] 2 p. l., 14 p., 1 l.

University of Illinois, 1917, PH. D.
"Extracted from the Tôhoku mathematical journal, vol. 13, 1918, edited by Tsuruichi Hayashi."

Henderson, Lawrence Melvin.

. . . The ratio of mesothorium to thorium . . . [New York, 1918] 13 p.

University of Chicago, 1916, PH. D.
"Private edition, distributed by the University of Chicago libraries, Chicago, Illinois."
"Reprinted from the Journal of the American chemical society, vol. XL, no. 9, September, 1918."

Hess, Raymond Washington.

The scale of influence of substituents in paraffine monobasic acids. The divalent oxygen atom . . . Easton, Pa., Eschenbach printing company, 1918. 26 p., 1 l.

University of Illinois, 1916, PH. D.

Hicks, John Frederick Gross, 1884–

The preparation and properties of yttrium mixed metal . . . [Easton, Pa., 1918] 9, [1] p., 1 l.

University of Illinois, 1918, PH. D.
"Reprinted from the Journal of the American chemical society, vol. XL, no. 11, page 1619."

Higley, Ruth, 1885–

Morphology and biology of some *Turbellaria* from the Mississippi basin . . . [Urbana, 1918] 1 p. l., [5]–94 p., 1 l.

University of Illinois, 1917, PH. D.
Published also as Illinois biological monographs, vol. IV, no. 3, January, 1918.
"Contributions from the Zoological laboratory of the University of Illinois under the direction of Henry B. Ward, no. 112."

Hotz, Henry Gustave, 1880–

First year algebra scales . . .   New York city, Teachers college, Columbia university, 1918.   3 p. l., 87, [1] p.

Columbia university, 1918, PH. D.

Huber, Harry Lee.

. . . The pharmacology and toxicology of copper salts of amino acids . . . [Baltimore, 1918]   1 p. l., p. 303–329.

University of Chicago, 1917, PH. D.

"Private edition, distributed by the University of Chicago libraries, Chicago, Illinois."

"Reprinted from the Journal of pharmacology and experimental therapeutics, vol. XI, no. 4, May, 1918."

Hufford, Mason Edward.

The diffraction ring pattern in the shadow of a circular object . . . [Lancaster, Pa., and Ithaca, N. Y., 1916] cover-title, p. [545]–550.

Indiana university, 1916, PH. D.

Without thesis note.

"Reprinted from the Physical review, n. s., vol. VII, no. 5, May, 1916."

Jackson, Thomas Franklin.

The description and stratigraphic relationships of fossil plants from the lower Pennsylvanian rocks of Indiana . . . [Indianapolis, 1917]   p. 405–428.

Indiana university, 1916, PH. D.

Without thesis note.

Reprinted from the Proceedings of the Indiana academy of science, 1916.

Job, Thesle Theodore.

Lymphatico-venous communications in the common rat and their significance . . . [Baltimore, 1918]   cover-title, p. 467–491.

University of Iowa, 1917, PH. D.

Without thesis note.

"Author's abstract of this paper issued by the [Wistar institute] Bibliographic service, August 15."

"Reprinted from the American journal of anatomy, vol. 24, no. 4, November, 1918."

Kahn, Reuben Leon.

Complement fixation with protein substances . . . [Baltimore, 1918]   1 p. l., 17 p.

New York university, 1916, D. SC.

"Reprinted from the Journal of immunology, vol. III, no. 4, July, 1918."

Kendall, John Norman, 1891–

Abscission of flowers and fruits in the *Solonaceae*, with special reference to *Nicotiana* . . . [Berkeley, 1918] cover-title, p. [347]–428.

University of California, 1917, PH. D.
University of California publications in botany, v. 5, no. 12, March 6, 1918, with a special thesis t.-p. dated May, 1917, attached to the cover-title.

Kenney, Arthur Webster, 1891–

I. The equation of state of liquid ether. II. The technical preparation of perchloric acid from potassium perchlorate . . . [Cambridge, Mass.] Technology press, 1918. 18 p.

Massachusetts institute of technology, 1918, PH. D.
Abstract of thesis.

Keyes, Donald Babcock, 1891–

Equilibria involving cyanogen iodide and the free energy of cyanogen . . . [Easton, Pa., 1918] cover-title, p. [472]–478.

University of California, 1917, PH. D.
Thesis t.-p. attached to the cover of the reprint from the Journal of the American chemical society, vol. XL, no. 3, March, 1918, by Gilbert N. Lewis and Donald B. Keyes.

Knox, John Knox.

. . . Geology of the serpentine belt coleraine sheet, Thetford-Black Lake mining district, Quebec . . . Chicago, Ill., 1918. 73 p.

University of Chicago, 1917, PH. D.
· Private edition, distributed by the University of Chicago libraries.

Kraus, Ezra Jacob, 1885–

Vegetation and reproduction with special reference to the tomato . . . by Ezra Jacob Kraus and Henry Reist Kraybill . . . [Corvallis, Or., 1918] 2 p. l., 3–90 p.

University of Chicago, 1917, PH. D.
"This bulletin is the result of the cooperative efforts of Messrs. Kraus and Kraybill and has been submitted by them in fulfillment of the thesis requirements for the degree of doctor of philosophy from the University of Chicago."
"Private edition, distributed by the University of Chicago libraries, Chicago, Illinois."
"Reprinted from station bulletin 149, Oregon agricultural college, January, 1918."

Kraybill, Henry Reist *see* **Kraus, Ezra Jacob.**

Kremers, Harry Cleveland.
Observations on the rare earths: the purification and
atomic weight of dysprosium . . . [Urbana? 1918] 22 p.,
1 l.
University of Illinois, 1917, PH. D.

Larsell, Olof, 1886–
Studies on the nervus terminalis: mammals . . . [Phila-
delphia, 1918] 68 p.
Northwestern university, 1918, PH. D.
"Reprinted from the Journal of comparative neurology, vol. 30, no. 1,
December, 1918."
"Author's abstract of this paper issued by the [Wistar institute] Biblio-
graphic service, December 9."

Leman, Edwin Daniel.
. . . The relation between the alpha-ray activities and
ranges of radioactive substances . . . Chicago, Ill., 1918.
2 p. l., 20 p.
University of Chicago, 1915, PH. D.
"Private edition, distributed by the University of Chicago libraries."

Lindstrom, Ernest Walter, 1891–
Chlorophyll inheritance in maize . . . [Ithaca, 1918]
68 p.
Cornell university, 1918, PH. D.
"Reprint from the Cornell university experiment station Memoir 13,
August, 1918."
"Paper no. 65, Department of plant breeding, Cornell university, Ithaca,
New York."

Luckey, Bertha Musson.
The specific brightness of colors . . . Lincoln, 1916. 60 p.
University of Nebraska, 1916, PH. D.

Ludwig, Clinton Albert, 1886–
The influence of illuminating gas and its constituents on
certain bacteria and fungi . . . Lancaster, Pa., Press of the
New era printing company, 1918. 1 p. l., 31 p.
University of Michigan, 1917, PH. D.
"Reprinted from the American journal of botany, 5: 1–31, January,
1918."
"Publication no. 167 from the Botanical department of the University
of Michigan."

McClugage, Harry Bruce.

Experiments on the utilization of nitrogen, calcium, and magnesium in diets containing carrots and spinach, by Harry B. McClugage and Lafayette B. Mendel . . . [Baltimore, 1918] cover-title, p. 353–366.

"The data in this paper are taken from the dissertation presented by Harry B. McClugage for the degree of doctor of philosophy, Yale university, 1918."

"From the Sheffield laboratory of physiological chemistry, Yale university, New Haven."

"Reprinted from the Journal of biological chemistry, vol. xxxv, no. 2, August, 1918."

McCrosky, Carl Raymond, 1890–

The oxidizing action of potassium dichromate as compared with that of pure iodine . . . Columbus, O., 1918. 15 p.

Ohio state university, 1918, PH. D.

MacDaniels, Laurence Howland, 1888–

The histology of the phloem in certain woody angiosperms . . . Ithaca, N. Y., 1918. 1 p. l., p. 347–378.

Cornell university, 1917, PH. D.

"Reprinted from the American journal of botany, 5 . . . July, 1918."

McEwen, Robert Stanley, 1888–

The reactions to light and to gravity in *Drosophila* and its mutants . . . [Baltimore, 1918] cover-title, 49–106 p., 1 l.

Columbia university, 1917, PH. D.

"Author's abstract of this paper issued by the [Wistar institute] Bibliographic service, December 22."

"Reprinted from the Journal of experimental zoölogy, vol. 25, no. 1, February 1918."

McWhorter, Golder Louis, 1888–

Some clinical and experimental observations on gastric acidity use of the gas-chain method . . . [Philadelphia, etc., 1918] cover-title, 13 p.

University of Minnesota, 1918, PH. D.

Slip with thesis note mounted on p. 2 of cover.

"From the American journal of the medical sciences, May, 1918, no. 5, vol. CLV, p. 672."

Mahood, Samuel Arthur, 1884–

Tetraiodophenolphthalein and tetraiodophenoltetrachlorophthalein and some of their derivatives, by W. R. Orndorff and S. A. Mahood . . . [Easton, Pa., 1918] 1 p l., p. [937]–955.

"A reprint of an article based upon a thesis submitted to the Faculty of the Graduate school of Cornell university for the degree of doctor of philosophy, by Samuel Arthur Mahood." 1917.

W. R. Orndorff, instructor under whom thesis was written.

"Reprinted from the Journal of the American chemical society, vol. XL, no. 6, June, 1918."

Marcus, Joseph K., 1894–

The synthesis of mono-amino-flavones, of flavone-azobeta-naphthol dyes and of other flavone derivatives . . . New York, Chauncey Holt company [1918]   38 p.

Columbia university, 1918, PH. D.

Minnick, John Harrison, 1877–

. . . An investigation of certain abilities fundamental to the study of geometry . . .   Lancaster, Pa., Press of the New era printing company, 1918.   vii, 108 p.

University of Pennsylvania, 1918, PH. D.

Mohler, Fred Loomis, 1893–

Resonance radiation of sodium vapor excited by one of the D lines . . . [Lancaster, Pa., 1918]   1 p. l., [70]–80, [1] p.

Johns Hopkins university, 1917, PH. D.

"Reprinted from the Physical review, n. s., vol. XI, no. 1, January, 1918."

Morris, Harold Hulett.

. . . A study of the chemistry of gold at high temperatures and pressures . . . [Easton, Pa., 1918]   cover-title, p. [917]–927.

University of Wisconsin, 1917, PH. D.

Thesis note is a foot-note on p. [917]; also stamped on cover.

"Reprinted from the Journal of the American chemical society, vol. XL, LO. 6.   June, 1918."

Mortimer, Franklin Spencer, 1891–

The electromotive force and free energy of dilution of lithium chloride in aqueous and alcoholic solutions . . . Easton, Pa., Eschenbach printing company, 1918.   19, [1] p.

University of Iowa, 1917, PH. D.

Mullinix, Raymond David.
. . . I. The conductivity of alkaline earth formates in anhydrous formic acid. II. The manufacture of potassium manganate . . . Chicago, Ill., 1918. 13 p.

University of Chicago, 1918, PH. D.
"Private edition, distributed by the University of Chicago libraries."

Musselman, John Rogers, 1890–
The set of eight self-associated points in space . . . [Baltimore, 1918] 1 p. l., p. [69]–86, 1 l.

Johns Hopkins university, 1916, PH. D.
"Reprinted from American journal of mathematics, vol. XL, no. 1, January, 1918."

Muttkowski, Richard Anthony, 1887–
The fauna of Lake Mendota . . . [Madison, Wis.] 1918. cover-title, p. 374–482.

University of Wisconsin, 1916, PH. D.
Thesis note stamped on cover.
"Reprinted from the Transactions of the Wisconsin academy of sciences, arts, and letters, vol. XIX, part I."

Nakahara, Waro.
Studies of amitosis, its physiological relations in the adipose cells of insects, and its probable significance . . . Philadelphia [1918] 1 p. l., p. 483–525.

Cornell university, 1918, PH. D.
"Author's abstract of this paper issued by the [Wistar institute] Bibliographic service, January 12."
"Reprinted from the Journal of morphology, vol. 30, no. 2, March, 1918."

Nelson, Thurlow Christian.
On the origin, nature, and function of the crystalline style of lamellibranchs . . . [Boston, 1918] cover-title, p. 53–111.

University of Wisconsin, 1917, PH. D.
Thesis note stamped on cover; also found in foot-note on p. 53.
"Author's abstract of this paper issued by the [Wistar institute] Bibliographic service, April 20."
"Reprinted from Journal of morphology, vol. 31, no. 1, June, 1918."

Newell, Anna Grace, 1876–

The comparative morphology of the genitalia of insects . . . [Columbus, O., 1918] 2 p. l., p. 109–142.

University of Illinois, 1916, PH. D.
"Reprinted from the Annals of the Entomological society of America, vol. XI, no. 2, June, 1918."
"Contribution from the Entomological laboratories of the University of Illinois, no. 51."

Nichols, Harold William.

. . . Theory of variable dynamical electrical systems . . . [Lancaster, Pa., Press of the New era printing company, 1917] 1 p. l., p. 171–193, 1 l.

University of Chicago, 1919, PH. D.
"Private edition, distributed by the University of Chicago libraries, Chicago, Illinois."
"Reprinted from the Physical review, n. s., vol. 10, no. 2, August, 1917."

Paine, George Porter.

. . . Report on modes of air motion and the equations of the general circulation of the earth's atmosphere . . . Washington, Govt. print. off., 1918. 1 p. l., p. 311–323.

University of Wisconsin, 1918, PH. D.
Thesis note stamped on t.-p.
"Reprinted from Monthly weather review, July, 1918, 46."

Parr, Rosalie Mary.

The response of *Pilobolus* to light . . . [London, 1918] 1 p. l., [177]–205 p., 1 l.

University of Illinois, 1916, PH. D.
"Reprint from the Annals of botany, vol. XXXII, no. CXXVI, April, 1918."

Peck, Edward Bates.

An investigation of the reaction between antimony and solutions of sodium in liquid ammonia . . . Easton, Pa., Eschenbach printing company [1918] 15 p.

Clark university, 1917, PH. D.
Reprinted from the Journal of the American chemical society, vol. XL, no. 2, February, 1918, p. 335–347.

Pierce, William Dwight, 1881–

Comparative morphology of the order *Strepsiptera* together with records and descriptions of insects . . . [Washington, D. C., 1918] cover-title, 3 p. l., p. 391–501.

George Washington university, 1917, PH. D.
"No. 2242.—From the Proceedings of the United States National museum, vol. 54."

Pinney, Mary Edith, 1881–

A study of the relation of the behavior of the chromatin to development and heredity in teleost hybrids . . . [Boston, 1918] 1 p. l., p. 225–291, 1 l.

Bryn Mawr college, 1918, PH. D.
"Author's abstract of this paper issued by the [Wistar institute] Bibliographic service, August 7."
"Reprinted from the Journal of morphology, volume 31, number 2, September, 1918."

Pratt, Frank Randall, 1876–

Heats of dilution and their variations with temperature . . . [Philadelphia] J. B. Lippincott company, 1918. cover-title, p. 663–695.

Princeton university, 1917, PH. D.
"Reprinted from the Journal of the Franklin institute, May, 1918."

Price, Henry Ferris, 1884–

. . . Fundamental regions for certain finite groups in S_4 . . . [Baltimore, 1918] [1], [108]–112 p.

University of Pennsylvania, 1915, PH. D.
"Reprinted from American journal of mathematics, vol. XL, no. 1, January, 1918."

Ramler, Otto Joseph, 1887–

On the three-cusped hypocycloids fulfilling certain assigned conditions . . . Washington, D. C., 1918. iv, 22 p.

Catholic university of America, 1918, PH. D.

Rathbun, Mary Jane, 1860–

The grapsoid crabs of America . . . [Washington, 1918] cover-title, xxii, 461 p.

George Washington university, 1917, PH. D.
"Bulletin 97, U. S. National museum, January 25, 1918."

Rawlins, Charles Henry, 1889–

Complete systems of concomitants of the three-point and the four-point in elementary geometry . . . [Baltimore, 1918] 1 p. l., [155]–173 p., 1 l.

Johns Hopkins university, 1916, PH. D.
"Reprinted from American journal of mathematics, vol. XL, no. 2, April, 1918."

Ray, Arthur Benning, 1889–

The electrolysis of solutions of the rare earths . . . [Easton, Pa., 1918]   10 p.

Cornell university, 1916, PH. D.

"Reprinted from the Journal of the American chemical society, vol. XL, no. 1, January, 1918."

Rees, Edwin Arthur.

Heterogeneous equilibria between aqueous and metallic solutions. The interaction of mixed salt solutions and liquid amalgams. A study of the ionization relations of potassium and strontium chlorides in mixtures . . . [Easton, Pa., 1918]   2 p. l., 46 p., 1 l.

University of Illinois, 1918, PH. D.

"Reprinted from the Journal of the American chemical society, vol. XL, no. 12, p. 1802."

Rees, Maurice Holmes.

. . . The influence of pituitary extracts on the daily output of urine . . . [Boston, 1918]   1 p. l., p. 471–484.

University of Chicago, 1917, PH. D.

"Private edition, distributed by the University of Chicago libraries, Chicago, Illinois."

"Reprinted from the American journal of physiology, vol. XLV, no. 4, March, 1918."

Robbins, Wilfred William.

. . . Successions of vegetation in Boulder Park, Colorado . . . [Chicago, 1918]   1 p. l., p. 493–525.

University of Chicago, 1917, PH. D.

"Private edition, distributed by the University of Chicago libraries, Chicago, Illinois."

"Reprinted from the Botanical gazette, vol. LXV, no. 6; June, 1918."

"Contributions from the Hull botanical laboratory 238."

Roberts, Elmer, 1886–

Fluctuations in a Mendelian character and selection . . . Philadelphia, 1918.   1 p. l., 157–192 p., 1 l.

University of Illinois, 1917, PH. D.

"Author's abstract of this paper issued by the [Wistar institute] Bibliographic service, October 8."

"Paper no. 7 from the Laboratory of genetics, Department of animal husbandry, University of Illinois."

"Reprinted from the Journal of experimental zoölogy, vol. 27, no. 2, November, 1918."

Robinson, Charles Summers, 1885–

Some experiments on the manifestation of osmotic pressure with membranes of chemically inert materials . . . [Ithaca, N. Y., 1918]   cover-title, p. [99]–127, [153]–183.

University of Michigan, 1917, PH. D.

Reprinted from two articles by S. L. Bigelow and C. S. Robinson in the Journal of physical chemistry, vol. 22, 1918.

Rodebush, Worth Huff, 1887–

The freezing points of concentrated solutions and the free energy of solution of salts . . .   [New York, 1918] cover-title, p. [1204]–1213.

University of California, 1917, PH. D.

Reprint from the Journal of the American chemical society, vol. XL, no. 8, August, 1918, with a special thesis t.-p. dated May, 1917, attached to the cover-title.

Rogers, Agnes Low, 1884–

Experimental tests of mathematical ability and their prognostic value . . .   New York city, Teachers college, Columbia university, 1918.   v, 118 p., 1 l.

Columbia university, 1917, PH. D.

Published also as Teachers college, Columbia university.   Contributions to education, no. 89.

Root, Francis Metcalf, 1889–

Inheritance in the asexual reproduction of *Centropyxis aculeata* . . .   [Princeton, N. J., 1918]   cover-title, p. [173]– 206.

Johns Hopkins university, 1917, PH. D.

"Reprinted from Genetics 3."

Sampson, Homer Cleveland.

. . . Chemical changes accompanying abscission in *Coleus blumei* . . .   [Chicago, 1918]   1 p. l., p. 32–53.

University of Chicago, 1917, PH. D.

"Private edition, distributed by the University of Chicago libraries, Chicago, Illinois."

"Reprinted from the Botanical gazette, vol. LXVI, no. 1, July, 1918."

"Contributions from the Hull botanical laboratory 240."

Scholl, Clarence.

The radioactivity of Illinois waters . . .   [Urbana? 1918] 30 p., 1 l.

University of Illinois, 1916, PH. D.

Schuette, Henry August.

A biochemical study of the plankton of Lake Mendota . . . [Madison, Wis.] 1918. cover-title, p. 594–613.

University of Wisconsin, 1916, PH. D.

Thesis note stamped on cover.

"Reprinted from the Transactions of the Wisconsin academy of sciences. arts, and letters, vol. XIX, part I."

Shoemaker, Harry Melvin.

. . . A generalized equation of the vibrating membrane expressed in curvilinear coordinates . . . Lancaster, Pa., Press of the New era printing company, 1918. iii, 18 p.

University of Pennsylvania, 1918, PH. D.

Skinner, Glenn Seymour, 1890–

XVIII. Molecular rearrangements in the camphor series. The decomposition products of the methyl ester of iso-aminocamphonanic acid. A new reaction involving the formation of the methyl ether of a hydroxy acid . . . [Urbana? 1918]   31, [1] p.

University of Illinois, 1917, PH. D.

Sleator, William Warner, 1883–

The absorption of near infra-red radiation by water-vapor . . . [Chicago, 1918]   cover-title, p. 125–143.

University of Michigan, 1917, PH. D.

"Reprinted for private circulation from the Astrophysical journal, vol. XLVIII, no. 2, September 1918."

Smith, Herbert Johnson.

. . . On equilibrium in the system: ferrous carbonate, carbon dioxide and water. On equilibrium in the system: zinc carbonate, carbon dioxide and water. Equilibrium between alkali-earth carbonates, carbon dioxide and water . . . [Easton, Pa., 1918]

University of Chicago, 1917, PH. D.

"Private edition, distributed by the University of Chicago libraries, Chicago, Illinois."

"Reprinted from the Journal of the American chemical society, vol. XL, no. 6, June, 1918."

Sperry, Pauline.

. . . Properties of a certain projectively defined two-parameter family of curves on a general surface . . . [Baltimore, 1918] 1 p. l., p. [213]–224.

University of Chicago, 1916, PH. D.
"Private edition distributed by the University of Chicago libraries, Chicago, Illinois, 1918."
"Reprinted from American journal of mathematics, vol. XL, no. 2 April, 1918."

Stewart, Chester Arthur, 1891–

Changes in the relative weights of the various parts, systems and organs of young albino rats underfed for various periods . . . [Baltimore, 1918] 1 p. l., p. 301–353.

University of Minnesota, 1918, PH. D.
"Author's abstract of this paper issued by the [Wistar institute] Bibliographic service, February 2."
"Reprinted from the Journal of experimental zoölogy, volume 25, number 2, April, 1918."

Stewart, John Quincy, 1894–

The movement of momentum accompanying magnetic moment in iron and nickel . . . Lancaster, Pa., Press of the New era printing co. [1918] 1 p. l., p. [100]–120.

Princeton university, 1919, PH. D.
"Reprinted from the Physical review, n. s., vol. XI, no. 2, February, 1918."

Stock, Chester, 1892–

The Pleistocene fauna of Hawver cave . . . [Berkeley, 1918] cover-title, p. [461]–515.

University of California, 1917, PH. D.
University of California publications. Bulletin of the Department of geology, v. 10, no. 24. Issued April 23, 1918, with special thesis t.-p. dated May, 1917, attached to the cover-title.

Stout, Joseph Duerson, 1886–

On the motor functions of the cerebral cortex of the cat . . . Washington, D. C., 1918. cover-title, p. 177–229.

George Washington university, 1915, PH. D.
"Reprinted from Psychobiology, vol. I, no. 3, November 1917."

Swaine, James Malcolm, 1878–

Canadian bark-beetles, a preliminary classification, with an account of the habits and means of control . . . [Ottawa, 1918]   2 p. l., 3–143 p.

Cornell university, 1919, PH. D.
"Reprinted from Canadian Department of agriculture, Entomological branch, Bulletin 14, part II, 1918."

Tanner, Fred Wilbur.

A study of green fluorescent bacteria from water . . . [Baltimore, 1918]   2 p. l., 63–101 p., 1 l.

University of Illinois, 1916, PH. D.
"Reprinted from the Journal of bacteriology, vol. III, no. 1, January, 1918."

Tarr, William Arthur.

. . . The barite deposits of Missouri and the geology of the barite district . . . Columbia, Mo., University of Missouri, 1918.   2 p. l., vii–xi, 111 p.

University of Chicago, 1916, PH. D.
"Science series, vol. III, no. 1, the University of Missouri studies."

Taylor, Rood, 1885–

Hunger in the infant . . . [Minneapolis, 1918]   cover-title, 34 p.

University of Minnesota, 1917, D. SC.

Thrun, Walter Eugene, 1892–

Determination of various forms of nitrogen in bovine flesh, including the products of hydrolysis of some of the proteins . . . [Baltimore, 1918]   1 p. l., 22 p.

University of Missouri; 1917, PH. D.
"Reprinted from the Journal of biological chemistry, vol. XXXIV, no. 2, 1918."

Tressler, Donald Kiteley, 1894–

Solubility of soil potash in various salt solutions . . . [Baltimore, 1918]   1 p. l., p. 237–257.

Cornell university, 1918, PH. D.
"Reprinted from Soil science, vol. 6, no. 3, September, 1918."

Ulrey, Clayton T., 1884–

. . . An experimental investigation of the energy in the continuous X-ray spectra of certain elements . . . Lan-

caster, Pa., Press of the New era printing company [1918]
1 p. l., p. [401]–410, 1 l.

(Phoenix physical laboratory contribution no. 40)
Columbia university, 1918, PH. D.
"Reprinted from the Physical review, vol. XI, no. 5, May, 1918."

Ulrey, Dayton L., 1884–

The relation between the specific inductive capacity of
an electrolyte and the electric potential of a metal placed
in it . . . Lancaster, Pa., Press of the New era printing
company [1918] 1 p. l., p. [47]–58.

Leland Stanford junior university, 1917, PH. D.
"Reprinted from the Physical review, n. s., vol. XII, no. 1, July, 1918."

Valleau, William Dorney, · 1891–

Sterility in the strawberry . . . Washington, Govt.
print. off., 1918. cover-title, p. 613–670.

University of Minnesota, 1917, PH. D.
Thesis note mounted on p. 2 of cover.
"Reprinted from Journal of agricultural research, vol. XII, no. 10, Washington, D. C., March 11, 1918."

Veazey, John Armor.

Kathodo-fluorescence of crystals, by Thomas B. Brown.
Part I.—A quantitative investigation of the kathodo-fluorescence of willemite, kunzite, and soda glass. (A description of the results obtained by J. A. Veazey.) Part II.—
A further investigation of willemite by the writer . . .
Lancaster, Pa., Press of the New era printing company,
1918. 1 p. l., p. [39]–57.

"Part I is the substance of a thesis presented to the Faculty of the
Graduate school of Cornell university by J. A. Veazey for the degree of
doctor of philosophy."
"Part II is a thesis presented to the Faculty of the Graduate school of
Cornell university by Thomas B. Brown for the degree of doctor of philosophy." 1916.
"Since the untimely death of J. A. Veazey prevented the immediate
publication of his thesis, and since the work of the writer is so closely
related to this previous work, these two papers are here issued as a single
publication."
"Reprinted from Physical review, vol. XI, no. 1, January, 1918."

See **Brown, Thomas Benjamin.**

Vollweiler, Ernest Henry, 1893–

The action of acid halides on aldehydes and ketones . . . [Easton, Pa., 1918] 19, [1] p.

University of Illinois, 1918, PH. D.

"Reprinted from the Journal of the American chemical scoiety, vol. XL, no. 11, p. 1732."

Voss, Vivian, 1894–

The ratio of the intensities of the D lines of sodium . . . [Lancaster, Pa., Press of the New era printing company, 1918] 1 p. l., p. [21]–28, 1 l.

Johns Hopkins university, 1917, PH. D.

"Reprinted from the Physical review, n. s., vol. XI, no. 1, January, 1918."

Waksman, Selman Abraham, 1888–

Studies on proteolytic activities of soil microorganisms . . . [Baltimore, 1918] 2 pt.

University of California, 1917, PH. D.

Reprints from the Journal of bacteriology, vol. III, no. 5, September, 1918; no. 6, November, 1918, issued as thesis, with thesis t.-p. mounted on cover of pt. 1.

[Pt. 1] has title: Studies on proteolytic activities of soil microörganisms, with special reference to *Fungi*. [Pt. 2] Studies on the proteolytic enzymes of soil *Fungi* and *Actinomycetes*.

Warner, Earle Horace, 1889–

The pressure increase in the corona . . . Lancaster, Pa., Press of the New era printing company, 1918. 17, [1] p.

University of Illinois, 1918, PH. D.

"Reprinted from the Physical review, n. s., vol. VIII., no. 3, September, 1916; and vol. X., no. 5, November, 1917."

Waynick, Dean David, 1891–

The chemical composition of the plant as further proof of the close relation between antagonism and cell permeability . . . [Berkeley, 1918] cover-title, p. [135]–242.

University of California, 1917, PH. D.

University of California publications in agricultural sciences, v. 3, no. 8, July 12, 1918, with a special thesis t.-p. dated May, 1917, attached to the cover-title.

Weatherwax, Paul.

The evolution of maize . . . [New York, 1918] cover-title, p. 309–342.

Indiana university, 1918, PH. D.

Without thesis note.

"Reprinted . . . from the Bulletin of the Torrey botanical club 45 . . . September 9, 1918."

Weiland, Henry Joseph.
The measurement of the conductivity of electrolytes in very dilute solutions. . . . [Urbana? 1918] 25, [1] p.

University of Illinois, 1917, PH. D.

Weinstein, Alexander, 1893–
Coincidence of crossing over in *Drosophila melanogaster* (*Ampelophila*) . . . [Princeton, N. J., 1918] cover-title, p. [135]–159.

Columbia university, 1917, PH. D.
"Reprinted from Genetics 3 . . . March, 1918."

Weinstein, Israel.
Extracts of antibodies obtained from specific precipitates of typhoid-antityphoid serum complex . . . [Baltimore, 1918] cover-title, p. 17–33.

New York university, 1917, D. SC.
"From the laboratory of bacteriology and hygiene, New York university, New York city."
"Reprinted from the Journal of immunology, vol. III. no. 1, January, 1918."

Weiss, Charles.
. . . The properties of pneumotoxin and its probable function in the pathology of lobar pneumonia . . . [Boston, 1918] 2 p. l., p. 103–122.

University of Pennsylvania, 1918, PH. D.
With a t.-p. and dedication [1919?] prefixed.
"Reprinted from the Journal of medical research, vol. XXXIX, no. 1, September, 1918."

Welo, Lars Alvin, 1888–
On the variations of the photo-electric current due to heating and the occlusion and emission of gases . . . [Ithaca, N. Y., 1918] cover-title, p. [251]–276.

University of California, 1918, PH. D.
Reprint from the Physical review, n. s., vol. XII, no. 4, October, 1918, with a special thesis t.-p. dated May, 1918, attached to the cover-title.

Weniger, Wanda.
. . . Fertilization in *Lilium* . . . [Chicago, 1918] 1 p. l., p. 259–268.

University of Chicago, 1918, PH. D.
"Private edition, distributed by the University of Chicago libraries, Chicago, Illinois."
"Reprinted from the Botanical gazette, vol. LXVI, no. 3, September 1918."
"Contributions from the Hull botanical laboratory 243."

White, Edith Grace, 1890–

. . . The origin of the electric organs in *Astroscopus guttatus* . . . [Washington, D. C., 1918]   p. [139]–172.

Columbia university, 1918, PH. D.

"Extracted from Publication no. 252 of the Carnegie institution of Washington, 1918."

Whiteford, Gilbert Hayes, 1876–

A study of the decomposition of silicates by barium salts . . . Fort Collins, Colo., Courier press [1918]   26 p.

Johns Hopkins university, 1917, PH. D.

Wilson, William Harold, 1892–

On a certain general class of functional equations . . . [Baltimore, 1918]   2 p. l., 20 p., 1 l.

University of Illinois, 1917, PH. D.

Reprinted from American journal of mathematics, v. 40, no. 3, July, 1918, p. 263–282.

Woods, William Colcord, 1893–

The biology of alder flea-beetle . . .   [Orono, Me., 1917] 1 p. l., p. [249]–284.

Cornell university, 1917, PH. D.

Pt. I of thesis.

"Reprinted from Bulletin 265 of the Maine agricultural station."

Woods, William Colcord, 1893–

The alimentary canal of the larva of the alder flea-beetle . . . [Columbus, O., 1918]   1 p. l., p. 283–313.

Cornell university, 1917, PH. D.

Pt. II of thesis.

"Reprinted from the Annals of the Entomological society of America, vol. XI, no. 3, September, 1918."

Woodward, Alvalyn Eunice, 1884

Studies on the physiological significance of certain precipitates from the egg secretions of *Arbacia* and *Asterias* . . . [Baltimore, 1918]   1 p. l., p. 459–501.

University of Michigan, 1918, PH. D.

"Reprinted from the Journal of experimental zoölogy, volume 26, number 3, August, 1918."

"Author's abstract of this paper issued by the [Wistar institute] Bibliographic service, June 24."

Wright, Winthrop Robins, 1888–
The magnetization of iron in the absence of hysteresis . . .
[Lancaster, Pa., and Ithaca, N. Y., 1918]   cover-title,
p. 161–169.

> University of Michigan, 1917, PH. D.
> "Reprinted from the Physical review, n. s., vol. XI, no. 3, March, 1918."

Yocom, Harry Barclay, 1888–
The neuromotor apparatus of *Euplotes patella* . . .
[Berkeley, 1918]   cover-title, p. [337]–396.

> University of California, 1917, PH. D.
> University of California publications in zoology, v. 18, no. 14, September 7, 1918, with special thesis t.-p. dated December, 1917, attached to the cover-title.

Young, Charles Otis.
Tetrabromophthalic acid and some derivatives of tetra-bromophthalimide . . . Pittsburgh, Pa., 1918.   16 p.

> University of Pittsburgh,   , PH. D.
> "Reprinted from the Journal of the American chemical society, September, 1918."

Young, Vive Hall.
Some factors affecting inulase formation in *Aspergillus niger* . . . [Baltimore, 1918]   cover-title, p. 75–87, 114–133.

> University of Wisconsin, 1916, PH. D.
> Thesis note stamped on cover.
> "Reprinted from the Plant world, vol. 21, nos. 4 and 5, April and May, 1918."

Medicine

(Class R)

Benda, Theodore.
Mental factors in the causation, cure and prevention of disease . . . [Worcester? Mass., 1918]   90 p.

> Clark university, 1917, PH. D.

Cornell, Ethel Letitia, 1892–
A new clinical test for temperature sensitivity, a contribution to the study of temperature reaction in nervous diseases based on the reaction to simultaneous cold and

hot stimulation . . . New York, P. B. Hoeber, 1918. 1 p. l., 119–158, 335–372 p., 1 l.

Columbia university, 1919, PH. D.

"Reprinted from vol. I, no. 3 . . . and vol. I, no. 9 . . . The Neurological bulletin . . . °1918."

Eberson, Frederick, 1892–

A bacteriologic study of the diphtheroid organisms with special reference to Hodgkin's disease . . . New York city, 1918. 56 p.

Columbia university, 1918, PH. D.

Florence, Philip Sargant, 1890–

Use of factory statistics in the investigation of industrial fatigue, a manual for field research . . . New York, 1918. 156 p.

Columbia university, 1918, PH. D.

Published also as Studies in history, economics and public law, ed. by the Faculty of political science of Columbia university. vol. LXXXI, no. 3; whole no. 190.

Good, Harry Gehman, 1880–

. . . Benjamin Rush and his services to American education . . . Berne, Ind., Witness press [1918] . x, 283 p.

University of Pennsylvania, 1915, PH. D.

Published also without thesis note.

Hixson, Arthur Warren, 1880–.

A study of the conditions essential for the commercial manufacture of carvacrol . . . New York city, 1918. 2 p. l., 27, [1] p.

Columbia university, 1918, PH. D.

McWhorter, Golder Louis, 1888–

Some clinical and experimental observations on gastric acidity use of the gas-chain method . . . [Philadelphia, etc., 1918] cover-title, 13 p.

University of Minnesota. 1918, PH. D.

Slip with thesis note mounted on p. 2 of cover.

"From the American journal of the medical sciences, May, 1918, no. 5, vol. CLV, p. 672."

Moral, José D., 1885–

The action of certain antiseptics, toxic salts, and alkaloids on the bacteria and protozoa of the intestine of the rabbit . . . [New York? 1918] 12 p.

Columbia university, 1918, PH. D.

Woltman, Henry William, 1889–

Brain changes associated with pernicious anemia . . . Chicago, American medical association, 1918. cover-title, 56 p.

University of Minnesota, 1917, PH. D.
"Reprinted from the Archives of internal medicine, June, 1918, vol. XXI, pp. 791–838."

Agriculture—Plant and Animal Industry, etc.

(Class S)

Artschwager, Ernst Friedrich, 1889–

Anatomy of the potato plant, with special reference to the ontogeny of the vascular system . . . [Washington, D. C., 1918] 1 p. l., p. 221–252.

Cornell university, 1918, PH. D.
"Reprinted from Journal of agricultural research, vol. XIV, no. 6, Washington, D. C., August 5, 1918."

Bakke, Arthur Laurence.

. . . Determination of wilting . . . [Chicago, 1918] 1 p. l., p. 81–116.

University of Chicago, 1917, PH. D.
"Private edition, distributed by the University of Chicago libraries, Chicago, Illinois."
"Reprinted from the Botanical gazette, vol. LXVI, no. 2, August, 1918."
"Contributions from the Hull botanical laboratory 241."

Bradley, Harriett, 1892–

The enclosures in England, an economic reconstruction . . . New York, 1918. 3 p. l., 9–113 p.

Columbia university, 1917, PH. D.
Published also as Studies in history, economics and public law, ed. by the Faculty of political science of Columbia university, vol. LXXX, no. 2, whole no. 186.

Breitenbecher, Joseph Kumler.

. . . The relation of water to the behavior of the potato beetle in a desert . . . [Washington, 1918] 2 p. l., p. 343–384.

University of Chicago, 1913, PH. D.
"Private edition, distributed by the University of Chicago libraries, Chicago, Illinois."
"Reprinted from Publication 263 of the Carnegie institution of Washington."

Carsner, Eubanks.

Angular-leafspot of cucumber: dissemination, over-wintering and control . . . Washington, Govt. print. off., 1918. cover-title, p. 201–220, 3 l.

University of Wisconsin, 1917, PH. D.
Thesis note stamped on cover.
"Reprinted from Journal of agricultural research, vol. xv, no. 3 . . . October 21, 1918."

Clothier, Robert Waitman, 1871–

Farm organization in the irrigated valleys of southern Arizona . . . [Washington, D. C., 1918] cover-title, 4, 59, [1], 13, [1] p.

George Washington university, 1917, PH. D.
A reissue of United States Department of agriculture Bulletin no. 654, June 14, 1918, with 2 preliminary leaves and Addenda: Review of literature bearing on the subject (13, [1] p.)

Curtis, Otis Freeman, 1888–

Stimulation of root growth in cuttings by treatment with chemical compounds . . . [Ithaca, 1918] 1 p. l., p. 71–138.

Cornell university, 1916, PH. D.
"Reprinted from Memoir no. 14, August, 1918, of Cornell university agricultural experiment station."

Fenton, Frederick Azel, 1893–

The parasites of leaf-hoppers, with special reference to biology of the *Anteoninae* . . . [Columbus, O.] 1918. cover-title, [84] p.

(Ohio state university. Contributions from the Department of zoology and entomology. no. 51)
Ohio state university, 1918, PH. D.
Without thesis note.
Reprinted from the Ohio journal of science, vol. xviii, no. 6, p. 177–212; no. 7, p. 243–278; no. 8, p. 285–296.

Gardner, Max William, 1890–

. . . Anthracnose of cucurbits . . . Washington, Govt. print. off., 1918. cover-title, 68 p.

(U. S. Dept. of agriculture. Bulletin no. 727. Professional paper)
University of Wisconsin, 1917, PH. D.
Thesis note stamped on cover.

Giddings, Nahum James, 1883–

. . . Infection and immunity in apple rust . . . [Morgantown, W. Va., 1918] 71 p.

(West Virginia university agricultural experiment station . . . Bulletin 170, December, 1918)
University of Wisconsin, 1918, PH. D.
Thesis note stamped on t.-p.

Harvey, Rodney Beecher, 1890–

. . . Hardening process in plants and developments from frost injury . . . [Washington, 1918] 1 p. l., p. 83–112.

University of Chicago, 1918, PH. D.
"Private edition, distributed by the University of Chicago libraries, Chicago, Illinois."
"Reprinted from the Journal of agricultural research, vol. XV, no. 2, October, 1918."

Hawley, Ira Myron, 1884–

Insects injurious to the hop in New York, with special reference to the hop grub and the hop redbug . . . [Ithaca, N. Y., 1918] 1 p. l., p. 143–224.

Cornell university, 1916, PH. D.
Published as Cornell university agricultural experiment station Memoir 15, November, 1918.

Henderson, Martin Perry.

. . . The black-leg disease of cabbage caused by *Phoma lingam* (Tode) Desmaz . . .

(*In* Phytopathology, official organ of the American phytopathological society. Baltimore, 1918. v. 8, no. 8, p. [379]–431)
University of Wisconsin, 1914, PH. D.
Thesis note stamp added to caption title, p. [379] and also on cover

Hills, Thomas Lawrence, 1890– *

Influence of nitrates on nitrogen-assimilating bacteria . . . Washington, Govt. print. off., 1918. cover-title, p. 183–230.

University of Wisconsin, 1917, PH. D.
Thesis note stamped on cover; also found in foot-note on p. 183.
"Reprinted from Journal of agricultural research, vol. XII, no. 4 . . . January 28, 1918."

Hughes, Josiah Simpson, 1884–

. . . Some nutritive properties of corn . . . Topeka, Kansas state printing plant, W. R. Smith, state printer, 1918. cover-title, 3–39 p.

(Agricultural experiment station, Kansas state agricultural college. Technical bulletin no. 5)

Ohio state university, 1917, PH. D

Thesis note is a foot-note on p. 5.

Kendall, John Norman, 1891–

Abscission of flowers and fruits in the *Solanaceae*, with special reference to *Nicotiana* . . . [Berkeley, 1918] cover-title, p. [347]–428.

University of California, 1917, PH. D.

University of California publications in botany, v. 5, no. 12, March 6, 1918, with a special thesis t.-p. dated May, 1917, attached to the cover-title.

Kiesselbach, Theodore Alexander.

Studies concerning the elimination of experimental error in comparative crop tests . . . [Lincoln ? 1918] 95 p.

University of Nebraska, , PH. D.

"Reprint from Nebraska agricultural experiment station Research bulletin no. 13."

Kraus, Ezra Jacob, 1885–

Vegetation and reproduction with special reference to the tomato . . . by Ezra Jacob Kraus and Henry Reist Kraybill . . . [Corvallis, Or., 1918] 2 p. l., 3–90 p.

University of Chicago, 1917, PH. D.

"This bulletin is the result of the cooperative efforts of Messrs. Kraus and Kraybill and has been submitted by them in fulfillment of the thesis requirements for the degree of doctor of philosophy from the University of Chicago."

"Private edition, distributed by the University of Chicago libraries, Chicago, Illinois."

"Reprinted from station bulletin 149, Oregon agricultural college, January, 1918."

Kraybill, Henry Reist *see* Kraus, Ezra Jacob.

Lindstrom, Ernest Walter, 1891–

Chlorophyll inheritance in maize . . . [Ithaca, 1918] 68 p.

Cornell university, 1918, PH. D.

"Reprint from the Cornell university experiment station Memoir 13, August, 1918."

"Paper no. 65, Department of plant breeding, Cornell university, Ithaca, New York."

Roberts, John William.
. . . The sources of apple bitter-rot infections . . . Washington [Govt. print. off.] 1918. 26 p.

(U. S. Dept. of agriculture. Bulletin no. 684. (Professional paper))
George Washington university, 1917, PH. D.
Thesis note stamped on p. 1.

Rost, Clayton Ord, 1885–
Parallelism of the soils developed on the gray drifts of Minnesota . . . [Minneapolis ?] 1918. 68 p.

University of Minnesota, 1918, PH. D.

Swaine, James Malcolm, 1878–
Canadian bark-beetles, a preliminary classification, with an account of the habits and means of control . . . [Ottawa, 1918] 2 p. l., 3–143 p.

Cornell university, 1919, PH. D.
"Reprinted from Canadian Department of agriculture, Entomological branch, Bulletin 14, part II, 1918."

Tressler, Donald Kiteley, 1894–
Solubility of soil potash in various salt solutions . . . [Baltimore, 1918] 1 p. l., p. 237–257.

Cornell university, 1918, PH. D.
"Reprinted from Soil science, vol. 6, no. 3, September, 1918."

Valleau, William Dorney, 1891–
Sterility in the strawberry . . . Washington, Govt. print. off., 1918. cover-title, p. 613–670.

University of Minnesota, 1917, PH. D.
Thesis note mounted on p. 2 of cover.
"Reprinted from Journal of agricultural research, vol. XII, no. 10, Washington, D. C.; March 11, 1918."

Waldron, Ralph Augustus.
The peanut (*Arachis hypogea*); its history, histology, physiology, and utility . . . Philadelphia, Pa., 1918. cover-title, p. [301]–338.

University of Pennsylvania, 1918, PH. D.
Reprinted from University of Pennsylvania Botanical contributions, vol. IV.

Weatherwax, Paul.

The evolution of maize . . . [New York, 1918] cover-title, p. 309–342.

Indiana university, 1918, PH. D.
Without thesis note.
"Reprinted . . . from the Bulletin of the Torrey botanical club 45 . . . September 9, 1918."

Wells, Bertram Whittier.

. . . The zoocecidia of northeastern United States and eastern Canada . . . [Chicago, 1918] 1 p. l., p. 535–542.

University of Chicago, 1917, PH. D.
"Private edition, distributed by the University of Chicago libraries, Chicago, Illinois."
"Reprinted from the Botanical gazette, vol. LXV, no. 6, June, 1918."
"Contributions from the Hull botanical laboratory 239."

White, Earl Archibald, 1883–

A study of the plow bottom and its action upon the furrow slice . . . [Washington, D. C., 1918] 1 p. l., 149–182 p., 1 l., [2] p., 1 l.

Cornell university, 1917, PH. D.
"Reprinted from Journal of agricultural research, vol. XII, no. 4, January 28, 1918."

Wiggans, Cleo Claude, 1889–

. . . A study of some factors influencing fruitfulness in apples . . . Columbia, University of Missouri, 1918. 60 p.

University of Missouri, 1918, PH. D.
Reprinted from the Missouri agricultural experiment station Research bulletin 32.

Wilson, Benjamin Dunbar, 1888–

The translocation of calcium in a soil . . . . [Ithaca, N. Y., 1918] 1 p. l., p. 295–324.

Cornell university, 1918, PH. D.
"Reprinted from Memoir 17, December, 1918, of Cornell university agricultural experiment station."

Technology

Beatty, Albert James, 1871–

A comparative study of corporation schools as to their organization, administration, and methods of instruction . . . [Urbana? 1918] 116 p.

University of Illinois, 1917, PH. D.

Broderick, Thomas M., 1889–

The relation of the titaniferous magnetite deposits of northeastern Minnesota to the Duluth gabbro . . . Lancaster, Pa., Press of the New era printing company, 1918. 1 p. l., p. 663–696, 35–49.

University of Minnesota, 1917, PH. D.
Reprinted from Economic geology, vol. XII, no. 8, December, 1917; vol. XIII, no. 1, January, 1918.

Chen, Phoo Hwa, 1889–

An investigation of comparative deflections of steel arch ribs with three, two and no hinges . . . [Ithaca, N. Y., 1918] 2 p. l., 24 p.

Cornell university, 1917, PH. D.
Abstract of thesis.
"Reprinted from the Cornell civil engineer, vol. XXVI, pp. 184, 229, Feb. Mar., 1918."

Hughes, Josiah Simpson, 1884–

. . . Some nutritive properties of corn . . . Topeka, Kansas state printing plant, W. R. Smith, state printer, 1918. cover-title, 3–39 p.

(Agricultural experiment station, Kansas state agricultural college. Technical bulletin no. 5)
Ohio state university, 1917, PH. D.
Thesis note is a foot-note on p. 5.

Layng, Thomas Ernest.

Low temperature carbonization of coal and a study of the resulting tars . . . [Urbana? 1918] 34, [2] p.

University of Illinois, 1915, PH. D.

Mohlman, Floyd William.

The activated-sludge method of sewage treatment . . . [Urbana? 1918] 43, [1] p.

University of Illinois, 1916, PH. D.

Nagler, Floyd August, 1892–
Verification of the Bazin weir formula by hydro-chemical
gaugings . . . [New York, 1918] cover-title, p. [3]–54.

University of Michigan, 1917, PH. D.
From the Proceedings of the American society of civil engineers, vol.
XLIV, no. 1. Papers and discussions.

Putnam, James William.
. . . The Illinois and Michigan canal; a study in economic
history . . . Illinois centennial publication. Chicago, The
University of Chicago press, 1918. xiii, 213 p.

(Chicago historical society's collection, vol. x)
University of Wisconsin, 1909, PH. D.
Thesis note stamped on t.-p.

Roesch, *Sister* **Mary Jeanette,** 1884–
Vocational preparation of youth in Catholic schools . . .
Washington, D. C., 1918. 73 p.

Catholic university of America, 1918, PH. D.

Swann, Harvey Julian, 1884–
French terminologies in the making; studies in conscious
contributions to the vocabulary . . . New York, Columbia
university press, 1918. xxii, 250 p., 1 l.

(*Half-title:* Columbia university studies in Romance, philology, and literature)
Columbia university, 1918, PH. D.
Published also without thesis note.

Tarr, William Arthur.
. . . The barite deposits of Missouri and the geology of
the barite district . . . Columbia, Mo., University of
Missouri, 1918. 2 p. l., vii–xi, 111 p.

University of Chicago, 1916, PH. D.
"Science series, vol. III, no. 1, the University of Missouri studies."

Van den Broek, John A., 1885–
The effects of cold-working on the elastic properties of
steel . . . [London, 1918] cover-title, 41 p.

University of Michigan, 1918, PH. D.
"Reprinted from the 'Journal of the Iron and steel institute,' London,
England, of May, 1918."

Military Science

(Class U)

Mayer, Eli, 1880–
. . . War and religion; a sociological study . . . Philadelphia, Pa., 1918. 100 p.

University of Pennsylvania, 1918, PH. D.

Bibliography

(Class Z)

Ellinger, Esther Parker.
The southern war poetry of the civil war . . . Philadelphia, Pa. [Hershey, Pa., The Hershey press] 1918. 192 p.

University of Pennsylvania, 1918, PH. D.

Foster, Finley Melville Kendall, 1892–
English translations from the Greek; a bibliographical survey . . . New York, Columbia university press, 1918. xxix, 146 p., 1 l.

(*Half-title:* Columbia university studies in English and comparative literature)

Columbia university, 1918, PH. D.

Published also without thesis note.

Vollmer, Clement.
. . . The American novel in Germany, 1871–1913 . . . Philadelphia, International printing co., 1918. 3 p. l., [9]–94 p.

University of Pennsylvania, 1915, PH. D.

SECTION III

INDEX OF SUBJECTS

SUBJECT INDEX

References are made to the alphabetical arrangement in Section I. The numbers refer to items, not to pages. Numbers to which (Sup. 1914, 16, or 17) is added refer to the supplementary titles on pages 9–13.

Asexual reproduction: 274.
Aspergillus: 359.
Assessment of property for taxation: 195.
Association of voluntary movements: 32.
Asterias: 353.
Astroscopus: 345.
Atmosphere, Circulation of: 237.
Attainment of personality through culture and religion: 30.
Attention: 395 (Sup. 1916), 106.
Australia: 235.
Bacteria: 78, 194, 307.
Bacteria, Nitrifying: 148.
Bacteria, Pathogenic: 87.
Bacteriology, Soils: 107.
Bankruptcy, United States: 233.
Barite: 308.
Barium compounds: 346.
Bark-beetles: 304.
Basal connections of the tracheae of the wings of insects: 61.
Bavaria
   Church history: 146.
   Politics and government: 146.
Bavarian Illuminati: 295.
Bazin weir formula: 228.
Beaulieu, Eustorg de: 133.
Benzaldehyde: 19.
Benzoic acid: 2, 103.
Bible: 188.
Bible. Old Testament
   Samuel: 35.
   Jeremiah: 356.
Bible. New Testament
   John: 333.
   Epistles of Paul: 100, 288.
Binary forms: 260.
Bismuth: 8.
Bitter-rot infections: 268.
Black-leg disease of cabbage: 141.
Blessed Virgin Mary in early Christian Latin poetry: 139.
Botanical chemistry: 332.
Botany
   Abscission: 168, 278.
   Anatomy: 9, 199.

Botany—Continued.
   Colorado: 266.
   Ecology: 266.
   Embryology: 53.
   Galls: 339.
   Roots: 74.
Boulder Park, Colorado: 266.
Brain: 300, 351.
Brasses: 119.
Brightness of colors: 400 (Sup.1916).
Brightness sensibility of the retina: 28.
British Columbia, Geology: 55.
Brotherhoods, Teaching: 283.
Brownson, Orestes Augustus: 212.
Budget
   New York (State): 372 (Sup. 1917).
   United States: 251.
Business: 121.
Cabbage, Diseases and pests: 141.
Cables: 122.
Calcium: 349.
Calcium carbide: 19.
Calcium carbonate: 107.
California
   Paleontology: 298.
   Petrology: 77.
Camphor: 287.
Canada
   Employers' liability: 137.
   Fur trade: 75.
Canadian bark-beetles: 304.
Capture at sea: 256.
Carbonization of coal: 183.
Carrots: 197.
Carvacrol: 149.
Casa de contratacion de las Indias, Spain: 131.
Catholic church, Education: 272,283.
Catiline his conspiracy: 398 (Sup. 1916).
Cats: 300.
Catullus, C. Valerius: 284.
Cave fauna: 298.
Central America: 224.
Centropyxis aculeata: 274.
Cerebral cortex of cat: 300.
Chaucer, Geoffrey: 5.

Spermatozoa: 66.
Spinach: 197.
Spinal nerves: 68.
Spinoza, Benedictus de: 15.
Stage
    England: 52.
    Philadelphia: 44.
Standard of living in Japan: 220.
Stannic fluoride: 109.
State aid to public schools in Minnesota: 170.
State budget reform, 1911–1917: 251.
State citizenship: 156.
State governments: 90, 217.
State legislation concerning the free negro: 163.
State legislatures: 81.
State regulation of railroads in the South: 397 (Sup. 1916).
State regulation of the securities of railroads: 17.
State taxation: 195.
Steel: 319.
Steel arch ribs: 62.
Stelloids: 138.
Sterility: 318.
Stimulation of root growth: 74.
Story, Short: 241.
Stratigraphic geology: 84.
Strawberries: 318.
Strepsiptera: 247.
Sudermann, Hermann: 281.
Suetonius Tranquillus, C.: 153.
Suffrage, Negro: 250.
Suffrage, United States: 250.
Suffrage, Woman
    Iowa: 111.
    United States: 250.
Suggestive therapeutics: 26.
Sumptuary laws: 124.
Sunday-schools: 328.
Supernatural, Metaphysics of the: 165.
Swinburne, Algernon Charles: 142.
Synthesis of mono-amino-flavones: 205.
Syria, History: 177.
Sailors, United States: 301.

Tales, Hawaiian: 23.
Tars: 183.
Taxation
    China: 157.
    Delaware Co., Pa.: 330.
    United States: 93.
Taxation, State: 195.
Teaching brotherhoods: 283.
Technical education: 21.
Technique of narration: 241.
Technology, Terminology: 305.
Temperature: 25, 70, 110.
Tennessee, Geology: 84.
Terence: 186.
Testicle: 73.
Tetrabromophthalic acid: 358.
Tetraiodophenolphthalein: 204.
Textile fibers: 67.
Theater
    Germany: 88.
    Philadelphia: 44.
Theology: 150.
Theory of environment: 176.
Theory of groups: 253.
Therapeutics, Suggestive: 26.
Thermochemistry: 252.
Thermodynamics: 104.
Thetford-Black Lake mining district, Quebec: 175.
Thorium: 140.
Tiberius: 153.
Tidewater Maryland: 185.
Tirant lo Blanch: 317.
Toluic acid: 103.
Tomatoes: 178.
Touch: 105, 120.
Tracheae in arthropoda: 61.
Trade and navigation between Spain and the Indies: 131.
Tragedy, Greek: 374 (Sup. 1917), 211.
Training of the business executive: 121.
Transformations (Mathematics): 79, 260.
Translating: 281.
Translocation of calcium in a soil: 349.

SECTION IV

ALPHABETICAL LIST, BY UNIVERSITY, OF DOCTORS WHOSE THESES WERE PRINTED IN 1918

With Supplementary Lists, 1914, 1916, and 1917

ALPHABETICAL LIST BY UNIVERSITY
1914, FOURTH SUPPLEMENT

The date following the name indicates year degree was conferred.

BRYN MAWR COLLEGE

Harmon, Esther, 1912.

ALPHABETICAL LIST BY UNIVERSITY
1916, SECOND SUPPLEMENT

The date following the name indicates year degree was conferred.

COLUMBIA UNIVERSITY

Ferguson, Maxwell.

UNIVERSITY OF ILLINOIS

Clark, Helen, 1916.

INDIANA UNIVERSITY

Hufford, Mason Edward, 1916.

UNIVERSITY OF NEBRASKA

Luckey, Bertha Musson, 1916.

UNIVERSITY OF WISCONSIN

Coulter, Ellis Merton, 1917.

YALE UNIVERSITY

Harris, Lynn Harold, 1914.

ALPHABETICAL LIST BY UNIVERSITY
1917, SUPPLEMENT

The date following the name indicates year degree was conferred.

UNIVERSITY OF CHICAGO

Nichols, Harold William, 1919.

COLUMBIA UNIVERSITY

Keddy, John Lewis, 1919.

INDIANA UNIVERSITY

Jackson, Thomas Franklin, 1916.

UNIVERSITY OF MINNESOTA

Dodson, John Dillingham, 1918.

RADCLIFFE COLLEGE

Spring, Evelyn, 1915.

UNIVERSITY OF WISCONSIN

Blankenagel, John Carl, 1915.

194

ALPHABETICAL LIST BY UNIVERSITY, 1918

The date following the name indicates year degree was conferred; absence of date signifying that so far as our records show degree is not yet granted.

BRYN MAWR COLLEGE

Haseman, Mary Gertrude, 1918.

Pinney, Mary Edith, 1918.

UNIVERSITY OF CALIFORNIA

Abbott, Raymond Barrington, 1919.
Barrows, Albert Lloyd, 1917.
Bichowsky, Francis Russell von, 1916.
Bovard, John Freeman, 1917.
Bridgman, Olga Louise, 1915.
Brighton, Thomas Bow, 1917.
Clark, Guy Wendell, 1918.
Davidson, Gordon Charles, 1916.
Davis, Elmer Fred, 1917.
Eastman, Ermon Dwight, 1917.

Essenberg, Christine Elizabeth, 1917.
Estcourt, Rowland Metzner, 1916.
Kendall, John Norman, 1917.
Keyes, Donald Babcock, 1917.
Rodebush, Worth Huff, 1917.
Stock, Chester, 1917.
Waksman, Selman Abraham, 1917.
Waynick, Dean David, 1917.
Welo, Lars Alvin, 1918.
Yocum, Harry Barclay, 1917.

CATHOLIC UNIVERSITY OF AMERICA

Bast, Victor August, 1918.
Brockbank, Thomas William, 1918.
Heider, Andrew Bernard, 1918.
McCann, Mary Agnes, *sister*, 1918.
Michel, Virgil G.

Noel, Francis Regis, 1918.
Ramler, Otto Joseph, 1918.
Roesch, *Sister* Mary Jeanette, 1918.
Schuetz, John Joseph, 1918.

UNIVERSITY OF CHICAGO

Aronberg, Lester, 1917.
Ayres, Clarence Edwin, 1917.
Bakke, Arthur Laurence, 1917.
Beardslee, John Walter, 1913.
Behre, Ellinor Helene, 1918.
Breitenbecher, Joseph Kumler, 1913.
Buchholz, John Theodore, 1917.
Burwash, Edward Moore Jackson, 1915.
Cohn, Edwin Joseph, 1917.
Derieux, John Bewley, 1919.
Dudgeon, Winfield Scott, 1917.
Fortune, Alonzo Willard, 1915.
Fukuya, Shoan Masuzo, 1917.
Grant, Elmer Daniel, 1916.
Hanke, Milton Theodore, 1917.

Harvey, Rodney Beecher, 1918.
Hays, Heber Michel, 1915.
Henderson, Lawrence Melvin, 1916.
Hoashi, Riichiro, 1917.
Hobson, Elsie Garland, 1916.
House, Roy Temple, 1917.
Huber, Harry Lee, 1917.
Knox, John Knox, 1917.
Koller, Armin Hajman, 1911.
Kraus, Ezra Jacob, 1917.
Kraybill, Henry Reist, 1917.
Leman, Edwin Daniel, 1915.
Miller, Edward Alanson, 1915.
Mullinix, Raymond David, 1918.
Nourse, Edwin Griswold, 1915.
Parkins, Almon Ernest, 1914.

195

Porter, Kirk Harold, 1918.
Rees, Maurice Holmes, 1917.
Reuter, Edward Byron, 1919.
Robbins, Wilfred William, 1917.
Sampson, Homer Cleveland, 1917.
Slaten, Arthur Wakefield, 1916.
Smith, Herbert Johnson, 1917.
Sperry, Pauline, 1916.

Stuart, Henry Waldgrave, 1900.
Tarr, William Arthur, 1916.
Visher, Stephen Sargent, 1914.
Wardle, Addie Grace, 1915.
Watson, Arthur Clinton, 1915.
Wearing, Thomas, 1917.
Wells, Bertram Whittier, 1917.
Weniger, Wanda, 1918.

CLARK UNIVERSITY

Benda, Theodore, 1917.
Campbell, Ivy Gertrude, 1914.
McDougle, Ivan Eugene, 1918.

Mateer, Florence, 1916.
Peck, Edward Bates, 1917.
Smith, Frederick Madison, 1916.

COLUMBIA UNIVERSITY

Alexander, Thomas, 1918.
Balz, Albert George Adam, 1916.
Barnes, Harry Elmer, 1918.
Beckwith, Martha Warren, 1918.
Beegle, Frank Moore, 1918.
Blanchard, Julian, 1917.
Bradley, Harriett, 1917.
Childs, Hubert Guy, 1918.
Coombs, Helen Copeland, 1918.
Cornell, Ethel Letitia, 1919.
Davidson, Joseph George, 1918.
Dawson, Andrew Ignatius, 1918.
Dushkin, Alexander Mordecai, 1918.
Eberson, Frederick, 1918.
Engelhardt, Nickolaus Louis, 1918.
Florence, Philip Sargant, 1918.
Foster, Finley Melville Kendall, 1918.
Fox, Dixon Ryan, 1917.
Fundenburg, George Baer, 1919.
Garth, Thomas Russell, 1918.
Gowin, Enoch Burton, 1918.
Hale, Robert Lee, 1918.
Harvitt, Hélène Josephine, 1913.
Higby, Chester Penn, 1919.
Hixson, Arthur Warren, 1918.
Hotz, Henry Gustave, 1918.
Huang, Han Liang, 1918.
Johnson, Franklin, 1918.
Kahn, Lina, 1916.
Kent, Raymond Asa, 1917.
Kester, Roy Bernard, 1919.

Kraeling, Emil Gottlieb Heinrich, 1917.
Kruse, Paul Jehu, 1918.
Lamprecht, Sterling Power, 1918.
Le Duc, Alma de Lande, 1916.
Leffingwell, Georgia Williams, 1918.
Lowe, Boutelle Ellsworth, 1918.
Lowrey, Lawrence Tyndale, 1917.
McEwen, Robert Stanley, 1917.
Maddox, William Arthur, 1918.
Marcus, Joseph K., 1918.
Mead, Arthur Raymond, 1918.
Messer, William Stuart, 1918.
Moley, Raymond, 1918.
Moral, José D., 1918.
Noble, Stuart Grayson, 1918.
Northcott, Clarence Hunter, 1918.
Powell, Fred Wilbur, 1918.
Robinson, Mabel Louise, 1916.
Rogers, Agnes Low, 1917.
Rowland, William Tingle.
Sell, Lewis Lazarus, 1918.
Stauffer, Vernon, 1918.
Swann, Harvey Julian, 1918.
Tai, En-Sai, 1918.
Thurston, Henry Winfred, 1918.
Tucker, Robert Leonard, 1918.
Ulrey, Clayton T., 1918.
Vaeth, Joseph Anthony, 1917.
Weinstein, Alexander, 1917.
White, Edith Grace, 1918.
Zeydel, Edwin Hermann, 1918.

CORNELL UNIVERSITY

Adamson, William Augustus, 1917.
Artschwager, Ernst Friedrich, 1918.
Bowen, Ray Preston, 1916.
Bridgman, J. Allington, 1917.
Brown, Thomas Benjamin, 1916.
Chapman, Royal Norton, 1917.
Chen, Phoo Hwa, 1917.
Cole, Howard Irving, 1917.
Curtis, Otis Freeman, 1916.
De Porte, Joseph Vital, 1916.
Douglas, Gertrude Elizabeth, 1917.
Friedline, Cora Louisa, 1918.
Gaehr, Paul Frederick, 1918.
Garrett, Mitchell Bennett, 1910.
Goudge, Mabel Ensworth, 1914.

Hawley, Ira Myron, 1916.
Lindstrom, Ernest Walter, 1918.
MacDaniels, Laurence Howland, 1917.
Mahood, Samuel Arthur, 1917.
Martin, Asa Earl, 1915.
Nakahara, Waro, 1918.
Ray, Arthur Benning, 1916.
Swaine, James Malcolm, 1919.
Tressler, Donald Kiteley, 1918.
Veazey, John Armor.
White, Earl Archibald, 1917.
Wilson, Benjamin Dunbar, 1918.
Woods, William Colcord, 1917.

GEORGE WASHINGTON UNIVERSITY

Blumberg, Alfred, 1917.
Clothier, Robert Waitman, 1917.
Pierce, William Dwight, 1917.

Rathbun, Mary Jane, 1917.
Roberts, John William, 1917.
Stout, Joseph Duerson, 1915.

HARVARD UNIVERSITY

Greene, William Chase, 1917.
Haring, Clarence Henry, 1916.

Lutz, Harley Leist, 1914.

UNIVERSITY OF ILLINOIS

Baldwin, Francis Marsh, 1917.
Beatty, Albert James, 1917.
Crooker, Sylvan Jay, 1917.
Faust, Ernest Carroll, 1917.
Hebbert, Clarence Mark, 1917.
Hess, Ray Washington, 1916.
Hicks, John Frederick Gross, 1918.
Higley, Ruth, 1917.
Kremers, Harry Cleveland, 1917.
Layng, Thomas Ernest, 1915.
Mohlman, Floyd William, 1916.
Newell, Anna Grace, 1916.
Parr, Rosalie Mary, 1916.

Pasmore, Daniel Frederick, 1917.
Rees, Edwin Arthur, 1918.
Roberts, Elmer, 1917.
Sabin, Ethel Ernestine, 1916.
Scholl, Clarence, 1916.
Skinner, Glenn Seymour, 1917.
Stowell, Charles Jacob, 1917.
Tanner, Fred Wilbur, 1916.
Vollweiler, Ernest Henry, 1918.
Wang, Ching Chun, 1911.
Warner, Earle Horace, 1918.
Weiland, Henry Joseph, 1917.
Wilson, William Harold, 1917.

INDIANA UNIVERSITY

Weatherwax, Paul, 1918.

Wooley, Elmer Otto, 1915.

UNIVERSITY OF IOWA

Boyce, Myrna M., 1917.
Butterworth, Julian Edward, 1911.
Chang, Tso-Shuen, 1917.
Gallaher, Ruth Augusta, 1918.

Job, Thestle Theodore, 1917.
Mortimer, Franklin Spencer, 1917.
Pollock, Ivan Lester, 1917.

JOHNS HOPKINS UNIVERSITY

Bramble, Charles Clinton, 1917.
Campion, John Leo, 1917.
Freas, Raymond, 1917.
Greenfield, Kent Roberts, 1915.
Hamilton, Arthur, 1914.
Howell, Roger, 1917.
Kelly, Caleb Guyer, 1916.
Mohler, Fred Loomis, 1917.

Morimoto, Kokichi, 1916.
Musselman, John Rogers, 1916.
Rawlins, Charles Henry, 1916.
Root, Francis Metcalf, 1917.
Schaffer, Aaron, 1917.
Stockett, Joseph Noble, 1916.
Voss, Vivian, 1917.
Whiteford, Gilbert Hayes, 1917.

LELAND STANFORD JUNIOR UNIVERSITY

Ulrey, Dayton L., 1917.

MASSACHUSETTS INSTITUTE OF TECHNOLOGY

Felsing, William August, 1918.
Freed, Edgar Stanley, 1918.

Kenney, Arthur Webster, 1918.

UNIVERSITY OF MICHIGAN

Atwell, Wayne Jason, 1917.
Curtis, George Morris, 1914.
Garretson, William Van Nest, 1916.
Ludwig, Clinton Albert, 1917.
Nagler, Floyd August, 1917.
Robinson, Charles Summers, 1917.

Sleator, William Warner, 1917.
Snell, Ada Laura Fonda, 1916.
Snyder, Alice Dorothea, 1915.
Van den Broek, John A., 1918.
Woodward, Alvalyn Eunice, 1918.
Wright, Winthrop Robins, 1917.

UNIVERSITY OF MINNESOTA

Broderick, Thomas M., 1917.
Folsom, Donald, 1917.
Foote, Paul Darwin, 1917.
McWhorter, Golder Louis, 1918.
Norlie, Olaf Morgan, 1908.

Rost, Clayton Ord, 1918.
Stewart, Chester Arthur, 1918.
Taylor, Rood, 1917.
Valleau, William Dorney, 1917.
Woltman, Henry William, 1917.

UNIVERSITY OF MISSOURI

Thrun, Walter Eugene, 1917.

Wiggans, Cleo Claude, 1918.

UNIVERSITY OF NEBRASKA

Cornell, Clare Brown, 1915.

Kiesselbach, Theodore Alexander.

NEW YORK UNIVERSITY

Blechman, Nathan, 1917.
Kahn, Reuben Leon, 1916.

Taylor, John Prentice, 1917.
Weinstein, Israel, 1917.

NORTHWESTERN UNIVERSITY

Larsell, Olof, 1918.

OHIO STATE UNIVERSITY

Adkins, Homer Burton, 1918.
Bock, Carl William, 1917.
Fenton, Frederick Azel, 1918.

Hughes, Josiah Simpson, 1917.
McCrosky, Carl Raymond, 1918.

UNIVERSITY OF PENNSYLVANIA

Armstrong, A. Joseph, 1908.
Barron, Mary Louise, 1917.
Beckerman, Harry, 1918.
Blancké, Wilton Wallace, 1916.
Bossard, James Herbert, 1918.
Bowman, Howard Hiestand Minnich, 1917.
Brede, Charles Frederic, 1905.
Burchett, Bessie Rebecca, 1913.
Dodds, Harold Willis, 1917.
Ellinger, Esther Parker, 1918.
Ellingwood, Albert Russell, 1918.
Good, Harry Gehman, 1915.
Hamer, Philip May, 1918.
Hayward, Percy Roy, 1918.
Hollingsworth, William Wiley, 1918.
Holtzhausser, Clara A., 1918.
Ide, Gladys Genevra, 1918.
Jones, Paul Van Brunt, 1912.
Kephart, Adam Perry, 1918.
Lefferts, Walter, 1918.
Levi, Gerson Benedict, 1910.
Lonn, Ella, 1911.

Marvin, Donald Mitchell, 1918.
Mayer, Eli, 1918.
Minnick, John Harrison, 1918.
Moore, Charlotte, 1915.
Munro, Dana Gardner, 1917.
Musser, John, 1912.
Paschal, Franklin Cressey, 1918.
Paterson, Robert Gildersleeve, 1909.
Peters, Charles Clinton, 1916.
Phinney, Chester Squire, 1918.
Price, Henry Ferris, 1915.
Quimby, Mary Agnes, 1918.
Ridgley, Frank Harris, 1916.
Scholz, Karl William Henry, 1918.
Shoemaker, Harry Melvin, 1918.
Vollmer, Clement, 1915.
Waldron, Ralph Augustus, 1918.
Watkins, Gordon, 1918.
Weiss, Charles, 1918.
Wendel, Hugo Christian Martin, 1918.
Williams, Gertha, 1917.
Yerkes, Royden Keith, 1918.

UNIVERSITY OF PITTSBURGH

Young, Charles Otis.

PRINCETON UNIVERSITY

Amy, Ernest Francis, 1914.
Baldwin, Thomas Whitfield, 1916.
Furman, Nathaniel Howell, 1917.
Gordon, Newell Trimble, 1919.
Harding, Earle Atherton, 1918.

Henderson, Walter Brooks Drayton, 1915.
Lockert, Charles Lacy, 1916.
Pratt, Frank Randall, 1917.
Shafer, Samuel Robert, 1916.
Stewart, John Quincy, 1919.

UNIVERSITY OF VIRGINIA

Jacob, Cary Franklin, 1917.

WASHINGTON UNIVERSITY, ST. LOUIS

Bonns, Walter Weidenfeld, 1918.

UNIVERSITY OF WISCONSIN

Andrews, John Bertram, 1908.
Brandenburg, George Clinton, 1915.
Brann, Albert, 1918.
Carsner, Eubanks, 1917.
Cotterill, Robert Spencer, 1919.
Eller, William Henri, 1916.
Fulmer, Henry Luman, 1917.
Gardner, Max William, 1917.
Giddings, Nahum James, 1918.
Henderson, Martin Perry, 1914.
Hills, Thomas Lawrence, 1917.
Morris, Harold Hulett, 1917.

Muttkowski, Richard Anthony, 1916.
Nelson, Thurlow Christian, 1917.
Paine, George Porter, 1918.
Perlman, Selig, 1915.
Putnam, James William, 1909.
Quigley, Harold Scott, 1916.
Schuette, Henry August, 1916.
Sumner, Helen Laura, 1908.
Wann, Louis, 1919.
Whaling, Heiskell Bryan, 1915.
Young, Vive Hall, 1916.

YALE UNIVERSITY

Boström, Otto Henry, 1916.
Bruce, Harold Lawton, 1915.
Dunbar, Carl Owen, 1917.
Goad, Caroline Mabel, 1916.

Grout, Frank Fitch, 1917.
Hewitt, Theodore Brown, 1917.
McClugage, Harry Bruce, 1918.
Purcell, Richard Joseph, 1916.

CPSIA information can be obtained
at www.ICGtesting.com
Printed in the USA
BVHW04*0200230818

525056BV00011BB/765/P

9 780331 716641